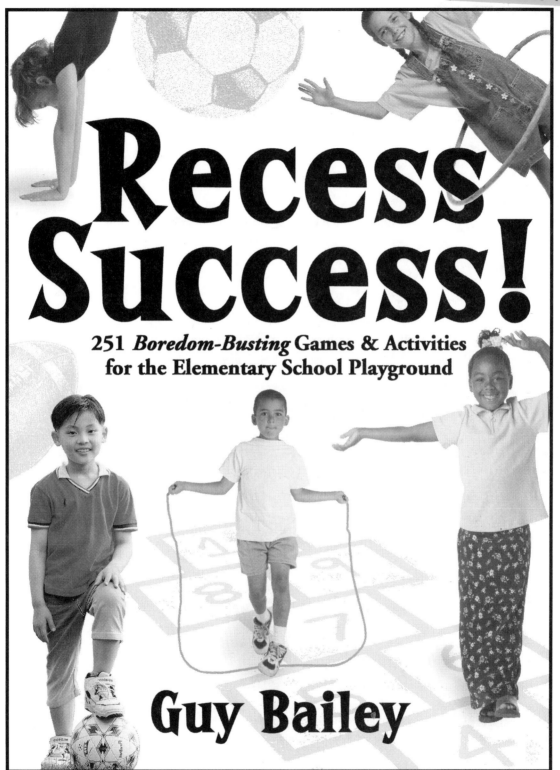

Recess Success!

251 *Boredom-Busting* Games & Activities
for the Elementary School Playground

Guy Bailey

EDUCATORS PRESS

Vancouver, Washington

ISBN: 978-0-9669727-6-4

Publisher's Cataloging-in-Publication
(Provided by Quality Books, Inc.)

Bailey, Guy, 1956-
    Recess success! : 251 boredom-busting games &
activities for the elementary school playground / Guy
Bailey.
    p. cm.
    Includes index.
    LCCN 2006909662
    ISBN-13: 978-0-9669727-6-4
    ISBN-10: 0-9669727-6-7

    1. Games--Handbooks, manuals, etc. 2. Physical
education for children. 3. Playgrounds. 4. Recesses.
I. Title.

GV1201.B235 2007   796.1
                              QBI06-600501

The author and publisher assume that the reader will teach these games using professional judgment and respect for
student safety. In regards to this statement, the author and publisher shall have neither liability nor responsibility in the
case of injury to anyone participating in the activities contained within.

EDUCATORS PRESS
15610 NE 2nd Street
Vancouver, WA 98684
(360) 597-4355
www.educatorspress.com

Printed in the United States of America

I dedicate this book to the thousands of students
who have walked into my gymnasium–and, into my life,
during my career as an elementary physical educator.
All of you have *greatly* enriched my life.

Acknowledgments

In writing *Recess Success!,* I must acknowledge a whole array of people. Over the course of my career, I have received numerous letters, phone calls, and e-mails from parents and school professionals about student behavioral problems and boredom during recess, as well as concern over the loss of recess in many of our nation's schools. This constant reminder made it clear to me that there was a need for this type of book. So to all of you who have voiced concern about the role of recess in our schools, and provided input on how to make it once again a fun and educational experience for children, I say thanks.

I must also thank all my colleagues in the physical education profession. Because some of the game ideas contained in this resource have been collected from attending workshops and conventions for over two decades, it is impossible to give specific game credit. However, I have learned so much from you in our sharing of ideas and teaching methodology over the years. Your professional advice, enthusiasm, and dedication to improving the health and fitness of our children is much appreciated.

Special thanks to the staff at Mill Plain Elementary School in Vancouver, Washington. Your feedback, encouragement, and support during the developmental stages of this book was invaluable, and all of you made this project a truly rewarding experience.

A special word of thanks goes out to all of my wonderful students who voluntarily played many of these games. I would have had few opportunities to try, modify, and create these games without them. Their exuberance for play and movement was a constant source of inspiration.

I would also like to acknowledge the many talented professionals that contributed to the design and production of this book. I am particularly indebted to Olga Melnik for her outstanding diagrams and illustrations. The setup and play procedures of each game in this book is made easier because of her gift at making games come "alive" for readers. I would also like single out Gerald Bergstrom for his masterful front and back cover design.

Finally, an author's family is always owed the greatest amount of gratitude, for they're the ones who make the biggest sacrifices. A special "Thank-you!" goes out to my four children, Justin, Austin, Heather, and Carson for their understanding, encouragement, and support.

Contents

Play is the chief business of the child.
It is the medium through which he expresses himself, and therefore if encouraged in right channels, play becomes educational. If parents and teachers properly understand the play of children, due recognition of its value will be given it in their daily life.

-Maude Cushing Nash

Preface

Recess Success! was written to solve the long-desired need for a game resource that would help create a safe, healthy, and peaceful playground setting for elementary school children. As one who has worked with children for over 24 years, I can assure you that most recess behavioral problems are the result of student boredom. And student boredom usually stems from a lack of knowledge regarding the game playing opportunities that are available at recess. This book addresses this problem through the use of fun and meaningful games that will provide a quality and invigorating recess experience for children in grades K-6.

In all, 251 games, sports, and play activities are included to meet the needs of a wide variety of student ages, interests, and skill proficiencies. There are games for both large and small groups, partner activities, sport games, traditional playground favorites, relay events, and even indoor games for rainy days. All of the activities can be used informally, or as a planned and integral part of the elementary physical education and recess curriculum.

Each game provides everything needed for its successful use. This includes an introduction, easy-to-understand directions, grade level suggestions, number of participants required, where to play, and equipment needed. Also included are helpful diagrams and illustrations to help you visualize the set-up procedures. In addition, you will find a full chapter devoted to explain the role and importance of recess, as well as information on how to use games most effectively in a school recess setting. This includes how to introduce games to children, finding the right game to achieve your play objectives, safety guidelines, and much more.

Recess Success! will have obvious appeal to school professionals such as physical educators, playground supervisors, and classroom teachers. However, this year-round resource will also benefit youth recreational instructors, camp directors, scout leaders, day care personnel, and parents. In fact, anyone who has faced the challenge of presenting game activities to children will find a treasure of exciting and useful ideas. The usage of these activities is unlimited and can serve game instructors in a variety of diverse situations.

The significance of recess and game playing in a child's physical, social, and emotional development cannot be overstated. Essentially, the school recess can represent a laboratory of real life for children. It helps children learn more about themselves and the world around them. It brings students together, fosters friendships, offers active participation leading to improved physical fitness, and gives them a much-needed reprieve from the everyday stresses of school. My desire is that *Recess Success!* provides you with a valuable tool for making this important part of the school day a quality learning experience—and, that it launches a lifetime of healthy play for your students. Have fun!

The real joy of life is in its play.
Play is anything we do for the joy and love of doing it.
It is the real living of life with the feeling of freedom and self-expression.
It is the business of childhood, and its continuation in later years
is the prolongation of youth.

- Walter Rauschenbusch

Using Games Successfully in the Elementary School Recess

There is a misconception in our society that the elementary school recess serves no *real* purpose—that, it is just "play" with no learning. In fact, recess and game playing are vital to a child's overall healthy development and can provide significant learning experiences. Besides participation in physical education (which, unfortunately, is not available in all of our nation's elementary schools), no other school setting has more potential for emotional, social, and physical development. The acceptance of recess as a critical learning opportunity is especially important considering the amount of time our children now spend pursuing sedentary and solitary activities with the computer, television, videos, and so forth. As a result, we now have children who are more overweight and physically unfit than ever before. Teachers, playground supervisors, school administrators, and parents have the opportunity to reverse this trend by offering play alternatives that can influence the behavior of children today—and, provide the skills for a lifetime of healthy play.

The Value of Game Playing at Recess

To best understand the value of game playing at recess, let's start by examining the many educational benefits behind their use.

- Game playing at recess creates a daily opportunity for healthy physical exercise. Recently, there has been an increased concern regarding the health and fitness levels of our children. As previously mentioned, the lifestyles of too many children include excessive television viewing, sitting at the computer, watching videos, eating junk food, and so forth. Time formerly spent playing active games with neighborhood friends is being spent at more sedentary activities. Recent studies have also shown a higher percentage of overweight children than ever previously recorded. This change in lifestyle has produced a nation of unfit children, many of whom are already saddled with significant cardiac risk factors. Many of today's young people are unaware of the necessity to be physically fit and lack the motivation to improve. The use of fun and meaningful game activities at recess provides a daily window of time to reverse this alarming trend and can help initiate healthful changes in young people that will enrich their lives. Enthusiasm and long-term motivation is critical to keeping kids moving—and, in the process, enhancing their skill and physical fitness levels.

- A direct correlation exists between exercise and classroom performance. Research has shown that children who participate in daily physical activities function at a higher level intellectually than those who do not. When children are deprived of vigorous physical activity, the heart isn't given the opportunity to pump fresh oxygen into the blood to nourish and stimulate the brain. Recess allows valuable time in the school day for children to participate in fitness enhancing activities.

- Game playing also offers children valuable opportunities to learn about competition. Since competition is an inherent part of our daily lives and in American society, games can provide wonderful "leading-up" lessons in sportsmanship etiquette and how to handle the emotional aspects of winning and losing. Competition can also bring out the best in a student when it is correctly approached. They learn how effort, persistence, and determination can affect the outcome of a game. This is especially true in game playing situations in which the student is encouraged by the instructor to concentrate on his or her personal performance rather than a final score against an opponent. In the school recess setting, the focus should on using competition to "improve," not to "prove." The teaching style of the instructor, more so than the game itself, is often the deciding factor in whether competition is a positive student experience or not.

- Game playing teaches children the skill of cooperation—that is, how to work together and how to help others. Through games, children can act out real life situations. They learn how to solve problems, look for alternatives, and resolve arguments. They learn how to work within defined guidelines and to accept the consequences if they do not. Recess games like tetherball, four square, and hopscotch encourage children to take turns. In the early grades, learning how to cooperate with a partner and others can be as difficult as competing in a meaningful fashion. In fact, without cooperation there would be no group games. Following the rules of a game and having the willingness to play with others requires cooperation. Since group competition is not possible without the skill of cooperation, the emphasis in the primary grades should focus on the skill of working together to achieve a common goal, as well as developing an appreciation and concern for teammates.

- Recess game playing can also be an excellent platform for learning social skills that carry on beyond the school playground. First, teach children to accept calls made by the instructor in a respectful manner (an integral part of any game situation). Also, encourage children to call infractions or penalties on each other and on themselves. Rather than having the game leader decide each issue, promote student negotiation and conflict resolution skills. Resolving differences, self-officiating, and learning how to self-organize a game are invaluable skills that will expand healthy play opportunities outside the recess experience.

- Through play, children can create a safe setting in which to develop friendships. In fact, the opportunity to play with friends is often the main reason why recess is the favorite part of a child's school day. This is especially true in rural or harsh weather areas where the chance to interact socially with others is limited. Additionally, recess provides a time to learn about schoolmates from various ethnic and social-economic backgrounds.

- Recess can provide a safe setting for children to test their emotional and physical capabilities. At their own pace, they can experiment with building relationships of the same and opposite gender, to feel what it's like to be a leader or a follower, to teach others or be taught, to play right field or be the pitcher, to chase or be chased, and so forth. Recess allows children the opportunity to master these mental, emotional, and physical obstacles that keep changing as their minds and bodies mature.

Although game playing provides the means to developing these skills, it is the game instructor who must create the learning opportunities. Instructors can make the most of this responsibility by organizing a recess program around games that are both skill-based and fun.

Achieving Specific Learning Objectives

Aside from the obvious fun and enthusiasm derived from game playing, there are two categories of educational benefits–*comprehension objectives* and *physical objectives*. Here are some of the specific benefits of game playing in each of these groups:

Comprehension Objectives

- Cultivating a respect for rules and procedures
- Learning the value of goals—as well as developing the patience and determination to accomplish those goals.
- Developing sportsmanship and an appreciation that one can compete against someone and still be a friend.
- Learning game concepts such as offense and defense
- Understanding the value of fairness and honesty
- Developing a cooperative attitude when working with others
- Discovering one's capabilities
- Developing patience and acceptance regarding one's limitations and the limitations of others.
- Cultivating readiness skills such as listening, following directions, resolving conflict, solving problems, and thinking strategically.

Physical Objectives

- Enhancing sport-specific skills in team and recreational sports
- Developing manipulative and fundamental movement skills
- Improving strength, speed, agility, flexibility, and body control
- Enhancing aerobic endurance
- Enhancing the use of spatial awareness skills by learning how to move safely within a group setting
- Developing eye-hand and eye-foot coordination

When choosing games for recess play, first define the play objectives you want to achieve. Naturally, different games emphasize different skills. Once you have decided on a specific learning objective, look for the game activity that best meets that objective and is developmentally appropriate for the age of your students. The physical, mental, and emotional levels of your students should also play a part in selecting appropriate games. In this book, you can find a game's objective in this text by simply looking at the introduction and purpose statement. There you will find what benefit(s) children will gain from the playing of that particular game.

Maximizing Participation

The strategy of maximizing participation to enhance learning is actually patterned after the inclusive style of teaching. It is based on the principle that every child should be included in the learning process 100% of the time at a level that meets his or her individual needs and abilities. A child cannot benefit from a game unless he or she is *actively* involved. In other words, during any specific instructional activity, including games, no child is excluded from learning, playing, or participating.

To give you an example of a typical non-inclusive game, let's look at the standby game of Steal the Bacon. In a traditional setting with twenty-six children, the instructor would divide the group into two teams and assign each child a number. Following regular play instructions, only two or four children are going to be active at any given time. The other twenty-something children are standing and waiting. Additionally, because the numbers are called at random, the children may be mismatched in their skill ability or size. In such instances, the disadvantaged children are subject to peer pressure and public ridicule. Unfortunately, the use of traditional recess games that exclude children from moving and learning is far too prevalent in the many elementary schools.

What can be done to change games so they become inclusive? First, consider changing and modifying the game rules, boundaries, and strategy. One of the easiest ways this can be done is to place children in pairs and/or small groups, and play several or multiple games simultaneously. Take the partner games listed in this book, *Soccer Duel* and *Football Duel*. In a large group setting of twenty-six children, there would be 13 games being played simultaneously. There are twenty-six children actively playing 100% of the time. As the physical education teacher, you can match up children according to their developmental levels to equalize each child's chance for success.

Other examples of modifying a game so it better meets the needs of your students are:
- Make the goals or boundary areas smaller or bigger.
- Change the requirements necessary for scoring.
- Increase the amount of equipment or number of balls normally used.
- Change the rules of an elimination game so that players return to action quickly.
- Eliminate certain penalties (as in the game of No Dribble Basketball—see page 40).

By changing the way a game is played, each child can be included in playing, learning, and experiencing success. However, despite the many virtues of small group and partner games, there will be times when an instructor will not be able to modify a game, and will need to use a more traditional large-group game. This might be due to a lack of equipment, supplies, play space, and so forth. This resource contains a section devoted to play activities specifically intended for those recess settings.

Guidelines for Teaching Games

Once you have chosen a game that meets your desired instructional objective, it is time to present it to your students. Here are some guidelines to use for teaching a lead-up game:

- Know the game well, including the strategy and student objectives, before introducing it to your students

- To minimize any wasted instructional time, have the players take positions in a starting position before explaining the rules.

- Be brief and to the point. Start with just enough rules to get the game started, then add other rules as the situation arises.

- Present game rules sequentially in small steps. Combine the oral explanation with a demonstration.

- Remind children of safety considerations associated with the game.

- Avoid situations where the children pick the teams.

- Before play is under way, ensure that the children have a sufficient understanding of the rules by allowing a time for questions.

- While play is under way, provide positive constructive feedback and appropriate encouragement. The feedback should highlight what is good about the student's performance, as well as what can be improved.

- To prevent confusion, have the players wear identification equipment such as vests, pinnies, flags, or armbands.

- Have a signal available that will immediately stop play if a dangerous situation should occur (for example, blowing a whistle).

- Again, stress enjoyment with competition based on "improving," not "proving." Help children understand that having fun and learning to perform skills correctly is more important than the outcome of the game.

After playing the game, use a question-and-answer session with the children to evaluate if specific learning objectives were met, and if the students understood and enjoyed the game. Use this feedback to determine your next instructional step. This feedback can also be used to change or modify a specific game so that it better fits the individual needs of your students.

Safety Considerations

In addition to teaching children the rules and strategy of playing a game, instructors need to teach safe play and provide safe playing areas. The following suggestions will help reduce accidents and injuries in your physical education program:

1. Conduct a visual scan of the play area to ensure that it is free of holes, posts, debris, or other obstacles.

2. Establish boundary lines that are far enough away from walls and fences so that children will not run into them.

3. Teach children to stop and start on given signals.

4. Make sure the children have sufficient spatial awareness skills before introducing games that involve tagging and chasing in a group setting.

5. Make sure the children are dressed properly. Require athletic shoes and prohibit the wearing of chains, dangling earrings, etc.

6. If possible, provide an adequate warm-up (including stretching exercises) prior to the playing of a game.

7. Model the safe use of any special equipment before the start of a game.

8. Use soft foam balls if a game involves the risk of students getting hit by a ball.

9. Place padding around any stationary equipment (such as volleyball or badminton net standards) in case students run into it during play.

10. Provide an atmosphere in which all students can feel safe and secure with each other. Intimidation and bullying behaviors should be dealt with a predetermined discipline plan.

It is the child in man that is the source of his uniqueness and creativeness, and the playground is the optimal milieu for the unfolding of his capacities and talents.

-Eric Hoffer, philosopher (1983)

How To Use This Book

Recess Success! contains 251 games, sports, and play activities to meet the needs of a wide variety of student ages, interests, and skill proficiencies. These activities are organized into eight sections to make finding an appropriate game easy and quick. The sections include traditional playground games, sport games, large-group games, small-group games, tag games, relay games, rope jumping activities, and indoor games for rainy days.

The explanations for each of the preceding games are organized in a user-friendly form that shows all the necessary information you need to know to present the activity to children. This includes:

- **Activity Title:** The title provides an idea of what the activity involves. For example, "Football Doubles" is two-on-two football game.
- **Introduction & Purpose:** Briefly explains the skill objective and play purpose of the activity.
- **Appropriate Grade Levels:** Tells what grade levels the activity is most successful with.
- **Number of Participants:** Tells you how many players are required for the activity.
- **Equipment:** Shows the kind of equipment needed. In the case of small-group and partner games, the amount of equipment is indicated for the number of participants in that particular activity. The total number of equipment needed will be dependent on the number of students in a class or at recess.
- **Illustration/Diagram:** Many of the activities will include an illustration or diagram to provide a visual representation of the play and set-up procedures.
- **How to Play:** Explains the set-up procedure and how to conduct the activity. Also, contains safety considerations and teaching hints.
- **Variations:** Gives ideas about how the activity may be modified or used in different situations.

To quickly locate a specific game by its title, you can go to the game index in the back of the book and find each activity listed alphabetically. You can refer to the appendix, also located in the back of the book to find additional information (resources, organizations, and web sites) regarding school recess, teaching strategies, physical fitness standards, playground safety, and more.

Playground Games

This section includes many of the classic playground games that have been played by children for generations. However, school professionals will also discover a variety of fun activities that contain a fun and new "twist" to the traditional favorites. Besides enhancing basic movement skills, these games will also keep kids active—thus, reducing the idle time that often leads to behavioral problems at recess.

Four Square

INTRODUCTION
This popular playground game develops striking skills and hand-eye coordination.

NUMBER OF PLAYERS
Four or more players to a court

EQUIPMENT
One playground ball for each court; for the Four Square game variations, refer to the specific game descriptions below for any equipment needed.

HOW TO PLAY
The court (a six-yard square) consists of four equal squares, which each square labeled A, B, C, and D. The server's square (A) has a service line marked diagonally across the square.

Each of the four players is assigned a square. The player in square A begins play as the server. The object of the game for the remaining players is to displace the player in square A, and to stay there for as long as possible.

The server, standing in back corner of his square, begins by dropping the ball and hitting it with an open hand into one of the other squares. The receiver can allow the ball to either not bounce or bounce only once before hitting it into another square. A player who misses, commits a foul, or fails to return the ball must move to square D, and the other players move up. If playing with more than four players, the player responsible for the error goes to the end of the challenge line and the first player in the challenge line moves to square D.

The five ways of committing a foul are:
1. Catching or carrying the ball.
2. Hitting a ball with a fist.
3. Hitting a ball out of bounds or landing it on a boundary line.
4. Allowing the ball to touch any body part except the hands.
5. Stepping into another square to play the ball.

VARIATIONS
There are many different variations to the traditional game of Four Square. Some of these include:

Around the World Four Square ———

This variation has the same rules of regular Four Square with one exception—the players must hit the ball in a certain direction. If the server begins by serving the ball to the right, then it must continue going around square-to-square in that direction. However, the server can call out "Left" and change the direction once the ball lands in his or her square. Play continues in this fashion until someone commits an error.

Beanbag Four Square ———

This variation is played like regular Four Square, except plastic scoops and a beanbag replace the use of a playground ball. Because this game requires catching a thrown beanbag (underhanded) with a scoop, the one-bounce rule does not apply. Fouls include (1) throwing the beanbag with an overhand motion, (2) throwing the beanbag out of bounds, (3) landing the beanbag out of bounds, (4) having the beanbag fall out of the scoop, (5) and touching the beanbag with anything other than the scoop.

Battle Four Square

Regulation Four Square rules apply in this game—unless, the server calls out "Battle" right before serving. When this happens, the server can hit the ball to anyone but the player receiving the ball must always hit it right back to the server. This continues until a player commits a foul or the server calls out "Battle Over." On this signal, the game resumes with regulation Four Square rules.

Catch Four Square

Regular Four Square rules apply, except players catch the ball instead of striking it. Players receiving a ball must let it bounce before catching it, and all throws must be made in an underhand motion. This is a particularly good game to play with the younger and/or less skilled students.

Doubles Four Square

This variation calls for eight participants. Have each student pair up with partner. Each pair is assigned a square with one player standing inside the square and the other waiting outside the square. Regulation Four Square rules are followed except partners will be switching in and out of their square throughout the game. As soon as the player standing inside the square hits the ball, he or she quickly moves out allowing the other player (who has been waiting outside the square) to step in. A foul by the partner inside the square results in both players moving to square D.

Team Four Square

With chalk, mark a court that is about twice the size of regular Four Square. Place an equal number of players (2-4 players) in each square. Unlike Doubles Four Square (see description on page 22), all teammates stay inside their squares without alternating turns. The rules and fouls are the same as in regular Four Square.

Paddle Four Square

This variation is played like regular Four Square, except paddles and a tennis ball replace the use of a playground ball. Instead of striking the ball with the hands, players use paddles. Fouls include (1) touching the tennis ball with anything other than the paddle, (2) allowing the ball to land inside one's square, (3) landing the ball on a boundary line, (4) hitting the ball out of bounds.

Four Square Tag

INTRODUCTION
This easy-to-understand game is much like Line Tag (see page 128), but now the lines of a regulation Four Square court are used.

NUMBER OF PLAYERS
Three to four players to a court; set up multiple courts for larger groups

EQUIPMENT
One foam ball

HOW TO PLAY
This game is played on a traditional Four Square court. Organize the players into groups of 3-4 players and assign each group to a court. One player begins as the "It," and stands on a court line with the ball (for tagging). The other players start by standing on a line anywhere around the court.

On a signal, the "It" chases and tries to tag one of the other players. All players, including the "It," have to stay on the lines while fleeing and chasing. A tagged player takes the ball from the "It" and becomes the new tagger. The "Its" are not allowed to throw the ball. The object of the game is to avoid becoming an "It."

VARIATION
If a Two Square court is available, consider playing **Two Square Tag.** The rules and play strategy are identical to Four Square Tag.

Four Square Swap

INTRODUCTION

This easy-to-understand and fun game can be played by children in a wide range of grade levels. Although the lines of a traditional Four Square court are used, the game strategy is unique and does not resemble the regular game of Four Square.

NUMBER OF PLAYERS

Five players to a court; for large groups, set up multiple courts and play several games simultaneously.

EQUIPMENT

None

HOW TO PLAY

This game is played on a traditional Four Square court. Organize the players into groups of 5 players and assign each group to a court. One player begins as the "It," and stands in the middle of the court. Each of the other four players start on a corner around the court.

Upon the "Swap" signal by the It, the four corner players must quickly switch places with each other. However, the It also tries to steal a corner. A player who first gets his or her foot on the corner is entitled to possession of that corner. The player left without a corner becomes the new It, and heads to the middle of the court for the next play. The game objective is to avoid becoming the It.

Four Square Team Tag

INTRODUCTION
This catch-and-tag game uses the lines of a regulation Four Square court.

NUMBER OF PLAYERS
Two teams of 3-4 players for each court; for larger groups, set up multiple courts.

EQUIPMENT
One foam or utility ball for each court

HOW TO PLAY
This game is played on a traditional Four Square court. Organize the players into equal teams of 2-4 players and assign two teams to a court. One team begins as the "Taggers," and start with the ball (for tagging). All players must be positioned inside the court.

The object of the tagging team is to tag and put out all of the members of the opposing team. On a signal, the team with the ball begins throwing the ball among themselves so that a member of the opposing team can be touched with the ball. The taggers can not move when they have the ball, nor can they throw it at an opponent. However, members of the tagging team can move when not in possession of the ball in order to set up a quick catch and tag of an opponent. A tagged player must leave the court, but he or she can re-enter the game if a member of the tagging team drops a pass or makes a pass out of bounds. In addition, a dropped or incomplete pass also results in the other team taking possession of the ball and becoming the taggers. The game ends when one team has successfully tagged and forced out all members of the opposing team.

Handball

INTRODUCTION

Like Wall Ball (page 34), this game is played with a wall adjacent to a paved or hard floor surface, and can be played with either a singles or doubles format.

This playground favorite develops striking skills and hand-eye coordination.

NUMBER OF PLAYERS

Either 2 or 4 players to a game; set up multiple play areas for larger groups

EQUIPMENT

One tennis ball for each court; chalk for marking boundary lines

HOW TO PLAY

This game requires a hard floor surface and wall. Mark off two out-of-bounds lines extending straight out from the wall that about 15-20 feet in width. A serving line, about 10 feet from the wall, should be marked from sideline to sideline. For singles play, assign two players to a court. For doubles play, organize the players into pairs and position two teams (a total of four players) to a court.

Singles (One against One). Designate one player to begin as the server. The server stands behind the service line and starts play by bouncing the ball once and hitting it underhanded against the wall. The opponent must return the ball to the wall before it bounces more than once. The ball is hit back and forth between the two players until one fails to hit the ball, lets it bounce twice, or hits it out of bounds. If the non-serving player makes an error, the server scores a point. If the serving player commits an error, then the next serve goes to the other player. Only the server can score points. The first player to score 21 points wins the game.

Doubles. Play is similar to Singles, except that there are now two players on each team. The partner closet to the ball returns it, and can hit the ball in succession (unlike Wall Ball in which partners are required to alternate hitting the ball). Also, only the serving partner may be in the court while serving, but his or her partner can run back in as soon as the serve is made. The scoring is the same as in Singles play.

Hopscotch

INTRODUCTION

There are as many Hopscotch diagrams and set of rules as there are countries! However, the game description and diagram shown below (Finnish Hopscotch) is the one most often used on school playgrounds in the United States.

NUMBER OF PLAYERS

Two or more players to a court

EQUIPMENT

One hopscotch court and one marker for each player (beanbag, stone, bottle cap, etc.)

HOW TO PLAY

Position the players in a file formation near space #1. The first player in line begins play by tossing his or her marker into space #1. The marker must land completely within the space. If it touches any lines, the player forfeits a turn and goes to the back of the line. If the marker lands correctly, the player jumps over space #1 and lands on one foot in space #2. The player proceeds down the court by hopping on one foot where a single space exists, and straddling the court where two spaces are side by side. When traveling to the last space and back, the player must stop at space #2 and pick up the marker from space #1 and hop out. If successful, the player proceeds on his or her next turn to throw the marker into space #2 and so forth. Players should take turns, always starting where they left off. The objective is to be the first player to complete the course.

A player forfeits a turn if any of the following fouls are committed:
1. Failure to throw the marker fully inside the intended space.
2. Stepping on a line.
3. Hopping into a space that contains the marker.
4. Using the hands for support while picking up a marker.

Kickball

INTRODUCTION
With its game strategy and rules, Kickball is very similar to the sport of Softball—and, a long-time favorite of children at recess.

NUMBER OF PLAYERS
There are normally nine players on a team

EQUIPMENT
Four bases, one playground ball

HOW TO PLAY
Set up a softball-type diamond as the playing field, with about thirty feet between the bases. Divide the players into two teams. Arrange one team on the field in fielding positions and line up the other team to kick. Ideally, you would have nine players on each side, positioned as in softball, but this can be modified depending on the number of players available.

The pitcher starts play by rolling the ball to the kicker, who is standing behind home plate. Foul kicks are counted as strikes, but a player can never get a third strike on a foul ball. If the kicker succeeds in kicking the ball into fair territory, he or she runs to first base. The fielders try to gain control of the ball and may put the runner out in one of three ways: (1) by catching a fly ball (that is, a ball kicked in the air), (2) tagging the runner with the ball, (3) or by throwing the ball to the first-base player who touches the base before the runner arrives. As in softball, throwing the ball to first base before the runner arrives is a "force" out, but the runner must be tagged when it is not a force situation at the other bases. A run (or point) is scored each time a base runner successfully circles the bases and touches home base.

Play continues with the sides changing after three outs. The team scoring the greatest number of runs after a predetermined number of innings wins the game. For safety reasons, the author does not recommend that fielders throw and hit a base runner for an out (as frequently allowed in some game settings). Rather, all outs should be made in the same way as regulation softball or baseball.

Tetherball

INTRODUCTION
This classic recess game enhances children's hand-eye coordination and agility.

NUMBER OF PLAYERS
Two players to a game; extra players can play if using non-scoring rules.

EQUIPMENT
One tetherball and a tetherball pole

HOW TO PLAY
A typical tetherball court is five feet in diameter, with a pole in the middle. For the scoring version, position two players to a court. In the non-scoring version, extra players can wait outside the court for a turn. Players must stay on their half of the court.

In the scoring version, the server begins by hitting the ball with the hand or fist in either direction. The opposing player attempts to bat the ball back into the opposite direction. Each player continues batting the ball back and forth, trying to wrap it completely around the pole in his or her direction. One point is awarded to the player who is successful at doing this. Play continues with the other player serving next. First player to reach 10 points wins.

In the non-scoring version, the player who is successful at wrapping the ball around the pole in his or her direction stays in the court. The other player goes to the end of the waiting line and is replaced by the first player in line. The objective is to stay on the court for as long as possible.

A foul will result in a free serve for the opponent, or loss of turn if using non-scoring rules. Fouls are called for the following:
- Stepping into the opponent's half of the court
- Playing the ball outside the court lines
- Hitting the rope
- Catching the ball (instead of striking it)
- Touching the pole
- Hitting the ball with any part of the body other than hands

Two Square

INTRODUCTION

This popular playground game develops striking skills and hand-eye coordination. It's also the perfect alternative to regular Four Square when only two players are available for a game.

NUMBER OF PLAYERS

Two or more players to a court

EQUIPMENT

One small playground ball for each court

HOW TO PLAY

The court (a six-yard rectangle) consists of two equal squares, which each labeled #1 and #2. The server's square (#1) has a service line marked across the back of the square.

Each of the two players is assigned a square. The player in square #1 begins play as the server. The object of the game for the remaining player is to displace the player in square #1, and to stay there for as long as possible.

The server, standing in back corner of his square, begins by dropping the ball and hitting it with an open hand into one of the other squares. The serve is made from behind the serving line. The receiver can allow the ball to either not bounce or bounce only once before hitting it back. If the server misses, commits a foul, or fails to return the ball, he or she must move to square #2, and the other player moves to the square #1. If playing with more than two players, the player responsible for the error goes to the end of the challenge line and the first player in the challenge line moves to square #2.

The five ways of committing a foul are:
1. Catching or carrying the ball.
2. Hitting a ball with a fist.
3. Hitting a ball out of bounds or landing it on a boundary line.
4. Allowing the ball to touch any body part except the hands.
5. Stepping into the opponent's square to play the ball.

VARIATIONS
There are many different variations to the traditional game of Two Square. Some of these include:

Beanbag Two Square ————————————

This variation is played like regular Two Square, except plastic scoops and a beanbag replace the use of a playground ball. Because this game requires catching a thrown beanbag (underhanded) with a scoop, the one-bounce rule does not apply. Fouls include (1) throwing the beanbag with an overhand motion, (2) throwing the beanbag out of bounds, (3) landing the beanbag out of bounds, (4) having the beanbag fall out of the scoop, (5) and touching the beanbag with anything other than the scoop.

Catch Two Square ————————————

Regular Two Square rules apply, except players catch the ball instead of striking it. Players receiving a ball must let it bounce before catching it, and all throws must be made in an underhand motion. This is a particularly good game to play with the younger and/or less skilled students.

Doubles Two Square

This variation calls for four participants. Have each student pair up with partner. Each pair is assigned a square with one player standing inside the square and the other waiting outside the square. Regulation Two Square rules are followed except partners will be switching in and out of their square throughout the game. As soon as the player standing inside the square hits the ball, he or she quickly moves out allowing the other player (who has been waiting outside the square) to step in. A foul by the serving team results in both players moving to square #2.

Paddle Two Square

This variation is played like regular Two Square, except paddles and a tennis ball replace the use of a playground ball. Instead of striking the ball with the hands, players use paddles. Fouls include (1) touching the tennis ball with anything other than the paddle, (2) allowing the ball to land inside one's square, (3) landing the ball on a boundary line, (4) hitting the ball out of bounds.

Team Two Square

With chalk, mark a court that is about twice the size of regular Two Square. Place an equal number of players (2-4 players) in each square. Unlike Doubles Two Square (see description at the top of this page), all teammates stay inside their squares without alternating turns. The rules and fouls are the same as in regular Two Square.

Wall Ball

INTRODUCTION
This classic playground game improves throwing and catching skills.

NUMBER OF PLAYERS
Either 2 or 4 players to a game; for larger groups, set up multiple play areas

EQUIPMENT
One ball small playground ball for each court; chalk for marking boundary lines

HOW TO PLAY
This game requires a hard floor surface and wall. Mark off two out-of-bounds lines extending straight out from the wall that about 10-15 feet in width. A short line, about 5 feet from the wall, should be marked from sideline to sideline. For singles play, assign two players to a court. For doubles play, organize the players into pairs and position two teams (a total of four players) to a court.

Singles (One against One). Designate one player to begin as the server. The server stands behind the short line and starts play by throwing the ball against the wall. The opponent must catch the ball before it bounces more than once; if not, the server receives a point and continues serving. If a successful catch is made, then he or she becomes the next server. Only the server can score points. The first player to score five points wins the game.

Doubles (Two against Two). Play is similar to Singles, except that there are now two players on each team. The two partners must alternate playing the ball. In addition, the two partners must alternate chances at serving. During play, any team that changes their alternating pattern of play loses the opportunity at serving. The scoring is the same as in Singles play.

34

Sport Games

Sport games bring a unique learning experience to the school playground. Participation in these activities can help children develop their physical skills—throwing, catching, dribbling, running, kicking, and coordination—and, enhance fitness levels and social growth. This section contains a wide variety of sports and modified team activities designed to help children develop these valuable skills—and, launch a lifetime of recreational enjoyment!

Basketball

INTRODUCTION
The basketball game description below contains regulation rules and strategies. However, modifying the equipment used by elementary-age students is highly recommended. For example, lowering basket heights and using smaller basketballs will help develop correct skill patterns, increase student success, and make the game more enjoyable. In addition to regular basketball, there are game alternatives listed below which emphasize skill development and fun.

NUMBER OF PLAYERS
Two teams of five players each

EQUIPMENT
One basketball, different colored vests

HOW TO PLAY
Regulation basketball is played on a rectangular court with a length of 94 feet and a width of 50 feet. There are two basketball backboards with goals suspended horizontally 10 feet above each end of the playing surface.

The game is played by two opposing teams of five players. A team is composed of two forwards, two guards, and a center. Players are not restricted to any part of the court and players can switch positions at any time.

The object of the game is to gain possession of the ball, to advance it into a scoring position by passing or dribbling, and to shoot and make a score by sending the ball through the opponent's goal. The team that does not have possession of the ball attempts to stop its opponents from scoring and tries to secure possession of the ball itself in order to score at the other end of the playing court. A field goal counts as two points. A free throw, given for a rule violation, counts as one point each. If desired, a 3-point line can be placed on both ends of the court, and any field goal made past the line counts as a 3-point field goal. After a score the ball is put back into play by the non-scoring team by a throw-in from the out-of-bounds line behind the basket.

A jump ball at the center circle starts the game. The official tosses the ball up between two opponents who jump as high as possible to tap the ball to a teammate. Each team then proceeds to gain possession of the ball and advance it toward the opponent's goal. A jump ball is also used during play when the ball is tied up between two opposing players.

A violation is an infraction which results in the ball given to the opponents at the out-of-bounds point near the spot of the violation. The following are violations:

- Causing the ball to go out of bounds by stepping on or over a boundary line while in possession of the ball, or passing or knocking the ball out.
- Traveling with the ball. Traveling is taking more than one step with the ball without dribbling, passing, or shooting.
- Kicking the ball intentionally
- Double dribbling the ball; that is, dribbling with two hands, or taking a second series of dribbles after having stopped the dribble.
- The offensive team taking more than 10 seconds to cross the centerline when moving from the back court to the front court. After crossing the centerline, a team may not return the ball to the back court unless touched first by an opponent.
- An offensive player staying more than 3 seconds in the key (the area inside the two sides of the free-throw line, the free-throw line, and the end of the court).
- Interfering with the basket on an opponent's shot (goaltending). Of course, this rarely happens at the elementary/middle school level.
- Taking more than 5 seconds for a throw-in from the out of bounds line.

A personal foul occurs when a player pushes, kicks, holds, blocks, hacks, charges, or engages in rough play. The player fouled receives two free throws from the foul line. If a player is fouled in the act of shooting and the basket is missed, the player receives two free throw shots. If the shooter made the field goal shot, despite the foul, the score counts and one free throw is awarded. On a missed free throw attempt, both teams are allowed to gain possession by getting the rebound. Any player with five personal fouls must exit the game.

A technical foul is given to a player or coach who acts in an unsportsmanlike way. The opposing team is awarded two free throws and ball possession afterward.

VARIATIONS

Instructors can adapt any of the rules to better meet the needs and ability levels of their students. For example, try reducing the size of the court, lowering the height of the baskets, using a smaller ball, eliminating some of the dribbling rules, etc.

Some basketball-type games that instructors might want to implement for the school recess program include the following:

Around the World ————————————————

This classic basketball game develops shooting skills from a variety of distances and locations around the basket. To begin, mark eight shooting spots (numbered one through eight) around the basket. Players decide a shooting order. The first player attempts to make a shot from spot #1. If successful, he or she moves to spot #2, and continues on as long as he or she is successful. When a player misses on the first shot, he or she has two choices. One choice is to not attempt a second shot. In this case, the player would wait for his or her next turn and would then shoot from that spot. The second option is to "risk it" and try a second shot attempt from the same spot. If the shot is made, the player continues. If missed, the player must start back at spot #1 on his or her next turn. The objective is to be the first player to make shots from all eight spots.

Basketball Pirates

This dribbling game does not require a regular basketball court, although a paved or hard surface is needed for dribbling. Designate several players to start out as the "pirates." The pirates stand without a basketball opposite the other players (the "dribblers") who each have a ball in hand.

On a signal, the pirates chase the dribblers and attempt to steal their basketballs. A dribbler who loses his or her basketball becomes a pirate, and the player who stole the ball now becomes a dribbler. The new pirate can not steal the ball from the player who just stole his or her ball. Additionally, no touching or fouling is allowed by pirates when attempting to steal. Dribblers must dribble continuously throughout the game using legal dribbling techniques. The objective is to last the game without becoming a pirate for as long as possible.

Basketball Dribble Tag

The skills of dribbling, ball control, and ball stealing are enhanced in this fun and easy-to-understand game. A regular basketball court is not required, although a paved or hard surface is needed for dribbling.

Designate several players to begin as taggers. The taggers stand without a basketball opposite the other players (the dribblers) who each have a ball. On a signal, the taggers chase the dribblers and attempt to tag as many as possible. Once tagged, a dribbler must stop and sit on his or her basketball. However, the tagged player can be freed if a dribbler touches him or her on the shoulder. Dribblers must dribble continuously using legal dribbling techniques. Select new taggers periodically throughout the game. The objective is to stay a dribbler for as long as possible without getting tagged.

Half-Court Basketball

Because it doesn't require a full court, Half-Court Basketball has long been a favorite on the school playground. Basically, the play area utilizes half of a regular court with just one basket needed. Form two equal-sized teams (three players each is ideal).

The game is played like regulation basketball with the following exceptions:

- A "throw-in" from the out-of-bounds line opposite the basket is used to start the game, and to re-start play after each score.
- During play, if the ball changes hands, the team gaining possession must take the ball past the extended free throw line before attempting a shot.
- There are no free throw shots for personal fouls. Instead, the team with possession throws the ball in from the nearest out-of-bounds line.

A team receives two points for each basket made.

39

Horse

This popular shooting game requires only one basket. Horse is best played with two to four players. Before starting, players must decide on a shooting order to be followed throughout the game.

The objective is to make a shot and hope the next player misses, causing the letters "H-O-R-S-E" to be eventually spelled against the opposing player(s). The first player begins by taking a shot from any place on the court. If missed, no letter is given but the next player in line is now allowed to shoot from a spot of his or her choice. If successful, each player in line must also make it from the same spot. Any player who misses gets the letter "H." A player only receives a letter if the previous player had made a shot and he or she missed it. A player is out of the game once "H-O-R-S-E" is spelled against him or her. Play continues in this fashion until one player remains.

Knock Out

This competitive game requires only one basket and develops shooting and rebounding skills. A group of three to five players is ideal for play. Players decide a shooting order and stand in a single file formation behind the free throw line. The first and second players in line start with a ball. To begin, the first player in line attempts a shot from the free throw line. If the shot is good, the player retrieves the ball and passes it to the next player in line without a basketball, and goes to the back of the line. If the first player misses the first shot, he or she retrieves the ball and keeps trying to make a basket from anywhere on the court. Meanwhile, the second player takes his or her free throw shot immediately after the first player's ball hits the floor. This player's objective is to "knockout" the previous player by making a basket before he or she does. A player who does not make a basket before the player behind him or her does has to hand the ball to the next player in line and is not out of the game. The third player takes his or her shot immediately after the second player's ball hits the floor, and the game continues. Players who are successful continue to return to the end of the line and wait for their next chance. The game ends when only one player is left.

No Dribble Basketball

Dribbling is a difficult skill to master for many young players (especially in a competitive game setting). Because of this, this game is a great way of allowing younger and less-skilled players a chance to play basketball without the pressure of dribbling.

This game is played on a regular basketball court. Form two teams of five players each. Although a jump ball is normally used to start the game, the instructor can simply designate one team to start on offense. The object of the game is to gain possession of the ball, advance it into scoring position by passing only, and to shoot and make a score (two points) by making a basket at the opponent's goal.

Regular basketball rules are used with the following exceptions:

- No dribbling is allowed (nor can a player walk or run with the ball).
- A player in possession of the ball has only five seconds to pass or shoot.
- Defensive players are not allowed to swipe the ball from the hands of an offensive player.
- A violation results in the ball given to the opponents at the spot of the infraction.
- There are no free throw shots for fouls (instead, the ball is given to the opponents).

One-on-One-on-One Basketball

This fun half-court game calls for three players; with each player being his or her own "team." Assign two players to start in defensive positions and one player on offense. The offensive player begins with a basketball at the top of the court.

The game begins with the offensive player dribbling toward the backboard in order to shoot and make a basket. The two defensive players work together to stop the offensive player from scoring. A defensive player who steals the ball or rebounds a missed shot becomes the new offensive player, and the previous offensive player now becomes one of the defensive players. If an offensive player successfully makes a basket, he or she continues on offense with possession of the ball at the top of the court.

A dribbling violation results in a jump ball between the two defensive players. In this case, the offensive player tosses the ball up in the air between the two defensive players. The offensive player cannot gain possession on a jump ball.

A fouled player retains possession of the ball at the spot of the foul. There are no free throws.

Each basket counts as two points. The objective is to end the game with more points than the two opponents.

Three Team Basketball

This game is played using half a court (one basket). Form three teams, each with three to fours players. Place two teams on the court ready to play each other, with the third team standing off to the sideline. Designate one team to start with the ball.

Like Half-Court Basketball (see page 39), the game begins with the offensive team throwing the ball in from the out-of-bounds line opposite the basket. In fact, play is exactly like Half-Court Basketball, except after each score the non-scoring team exits the court and the waiting team enters and starts on defense. The scoring team always retains possession and begins the next game with a throw-in from the out-of-bounds line opposite the basket. Play continues in this fashion with the teams keeping track of their scores. At the conclusion of play, the team with the most points is declared the winner.

Twenty-One

This is another shooting game that children love to play and requires only one basket. A group of three to five players is ideal for play. Players decide a shooting order and stand in a single file formation behind the free throw line. The first player in line begins with the ball.

To begin, the first player attempts a long shot and a follow-up shot. The long shot, if made, counts as two points and the follow-up shot counts as one point. The follow-up shot must be made from the spot where the ball was recovered (from the first shot attempt). After both shot attempts, the ball is handed to the next player in line who does the same. The objective is to the first player to reach exactly 21 points. Since a score of *over* 21 points results in a player having to start all over again at zero, a player needs to be careful which shots he or she makes or deliberately misses toward the end of play.

Flag Football

INTRODUCTION
Flag Football allows students to participate in a safer version of football while still retaining many of the passing, catching, and kicking skills used in regular football. If flags are not available, substitute a two-hand tag as a way to "tackle."

NUMBER OF PLAYERS
Two teams of seven players each

EQUIPMENT
One football, flags sets, kicking tee

HOW TO PLAY
At the elementary level, flag football can be played on a field of various sizes. However, a play area of 30 yards by 60 yards will be ideal for most grade levels. Form two teams of seven players. Each player is required to wear flags (one on each hip) for tackling purposes. The game leader should conduct a coin toss to determine which team will kickoff first. The team winning the coin toss has the option of which end it will defend, or choosing to kick or receive.

The game is started with a kickoff from the center of the field. All members of the kicking team must be onside. The kick must travel at least 10 yards or it does not count. A member of the receiving team wants to catch the kicked ball and advance it toward the opponent's goal line as close as possible before being downed. The kickoff may not be recovered by the kicking team unless fumbled by a receiver. A ball that is kicked out of bounds, and not touched by the receiving team, must be kicked again. A second consecutive kick out of bounds gives the receiving team the ball at the center of the field.

The offensive team has four downs to advance the ball from the point of possession forward 10 yards or they lose the ball. If successful, they are given four additional downs. If not successful, the ball is awarded to the opponents on the spot where the last play ended.

Before each play, the offensive team is allowed to huddle for 30 seconds to make up a play. If seven players are on a team, three players are required to be on the line of scrimmage prior to the start of the play. The offensive positions are as follows: left end, center, right end, left halfback, fullback, right halfback, and quarterback. The defensive team is not restricted to any particular formation.

During any play, a player carrying the ball who has at least one flag pulled is considered "downed." The tackler must pull the flags and cannot run into the ball carrier intentionally.

All fumbles are declared "dead" at the spot of the fumble. The first player who touches the ball on the ground is awarded the ball.

Blocking must be done with the arms and elbows close to the body. In addition, a block must be done from the front (it's illegal to block a defensive player in the back).

All forward passes must be thrown from behind the line of scrimmage, and all players are eligible to receive or intercept passes. A pass caught in the end zone scores a touchdown. A ball caught beyond the end zone is considered out of bounds (an incomplete pass).

The offensive team may elect to punt the ball rather than run or pass it. This option is used by a team when it is in danger of losing the ball on downs (that is, not having advanced the ball necessary for a first down). All punts must be announced ahead of time, and neither team can cross the line of scrimmage until the ball is punted. The returning team attempts to catch the ball and advance it toward the opponent's goal line until tackled. A forward pass can not be made on a punt return.

Running plays and forward pass plays that result in carrying the ball over the goal line into the end zone score a touchdown, and is worth six points. The team scoring a touchdown may receive an additional point (call a point after touchdown) by successfully kicking the ball through the football goalpost uprights from the 3-yard line, or by carrying the ball over the goal line on a run or pass (this option is worth two points).

A "field goal," worth three points, is awarded to an offensive team that successfully kicks a football through the goalpost uprights.

A "safety," worth two points, is awarded to a team that downs an offensive player while in his own end zone.

During play, a team is assessed a penalty of 5 yards for the following:
- Being offsides before the ball is put into play.
- Making a forward pass in front of the line of scrimmage.
- Delay of game (too long in the huddle).
- Playing without the flags in proper position.
- Failure to announce a punt.
- Using a stiff-arm or push off by the ball carrier.
- The offensive team having less than three players on the line of scrimmage.

The following penalties are assessed a 15-yard penalty:
- Unnecessary roughness (pushing, tripping, holding, tackling with the body, etc.)
- Unsportsmanlike conduct
- Illegal block (usually occurs when a players blocks another player in the back)
- Pass interference (when a player makes contact with a receiver before the ball has arrived)

The length of the game will vary. However, in general, four 10-minute periods constitute a game. At the end of play, the team with the highest number of points wins.

VARIATIONS

As mentioned in the game introduction, consider playing **Touch Football.** The rules of regular Flag Football apply— except no flags are worn. The ball is downed at the spot on the field where the carrier is tagged by a defensive player with both hands simultaneously.

Other football-type games that are appropriate for the school recess include the following:

End Zone

With cones, mark off a rectangular-shaped play area about the size of a basketball court. A center line is marked down the middle. The areas past the end lines are called "end zones." Divide the players into two equal teams (six to twelve players each). Position half of each team in their assigned end zone and half of the team on their side of the center line facing their teammates in the end zone. One of the players is given a football to start.

The objective is for a court player to complete a pass to a teammate in the end zone for a score. The game begins an end zone player in possession of a football. The end zone player tries to pass the ball to a teammate in the far court. During play, court players of both teams catch or retrieve the ball and attempt to complete a pass to a teammate in the end zone (worth one point). After each score or missed catch, the players in the end zone pass the ball back to their teammates in the court, and play continues non-stop. Court players can intercept or knock down pass attempts by the opposing team. At all times, both court and end zone players must stay in their designated areas. Periodically, add additional footballs to the game.

Football Duel

This simple game requires only two participants (each wearing flags), and can be played with a wide variety of grade levels. With cones, mark off a rectangular-shaped field about 30 feet by 60 feet in size. The two ends represent the goal lines. For large groups, just set up several play areas and play multiple games simultaneously. One player starts at each goal line. Designate one player to kickoff first.

The player with the ball begins by kicking the football off a tee toward the receiver. The receiver attempts to catch or retrieve the ball and run with it past the opposite goal line without having his or her flags pulled by the kicking player. If successful, the receiver scores a touchdown worth six points. The players switch roles after each play.

Football Doubles

For developmental learning purposes, Football Doubles is a natural progression from Football Duel (see previous game). Because this game requires two players on each team, the "team" concept of playing football is now introduced.

With cones, mark off a rectangular-shaped field about 30 feet by 60 feet in size. The two ends represent the goal lines. For large groups, set up several play areas and play multiple games simultaneously. Form two teams of two players each. Each player wears a flag on each hip for pulling. Designate one team to start on offense. The other team starts on defense, and places the ball in the middle of the field for a kickoff.

The defensive team starts the game by kicking the football off a tee toward the offensive players. One of the offensive players catches or retrieves the ball and attempts to score a touchdown by running it past the opposite goal line without having a flag pulled. The other offensive player (without the ball) blocks for the runner. If the runner is tackled, the ball is downed at that spot and the offensive team has one "down" (or play) to score a touchdown. To execute the play, one offensive player is the quarterback and the other is the hiker/receiver. The defensive team has one pass defender (who tries to stop the hiker/receiver from catching the pass from the quarterback) and one pass rusher. The rusher must wait for five seconds to pursue the quarterback after the ball is hiked. After the play, the teams reverse roles with a new kickoff (regardless if the offensive team scored or not).

Four Downs

This is a simplified version of regular flag football that requires fewer players. With cones, mark off a rectangular-shaped field about 30 feet by 60 feet in size. The two ends represent the goal lines. For large groups, set up several play areas and play multiple games simultaneously. Form two teams of four players each. Each player wears a flag on each hip for pulling. One team starts with the ball on their own goal line (there are no kickoffs). The other team starts on defense.

The offensive team consists of a quarterback, a hiker, and two receivers. The defensive team has three pass defenders and a rusher. The offensive team has four downs to move the ball down the field and score. Only pass plays are allowed. The quarterback is not allowed to run past the line of scrimmage, nor are there any handoffs. The rusher must wait for 5 seconds before pursuing the quarterback after the ball has been hiked. On a completed pass, the receiver runs toward the opponent's goal line until "tackled" by a defensive player (that is, the receiver has his her flags pulled). At that spot, the next play begins for the offensive team. An incomplete pass results in the ball being placed again at the same spot. If a team fails to score a touchdown after four downs, the ball is handed the other team and they begin on offense at their goal line (going in the opposite direction).

A touchdown (worth six points) is scored each time a ball carrier crosses the opponent's goal line with the ball, or a receiver catches a pass in the end zone.

No Ball Football

This is a great game for introducing younger children to the chasing and fleeing aspect of football, as well as to flag pulling ("tackling"). With cones, mark off a rectangular-shaped field that is about 50 feet long and 40 feet wide. The two ends represent the goal lines. Divide the players into two equal-size teams, and each team wear different colored flags. Designate one team to start on offense and to stand on their goal line. The defensive team lines up on the opposite goal line.

On a signal, the offensive players attempt to run through the defensive players to the opposite goal line. At the same time, the defensive players chase the offensive players and attempt to pull as many of their flags as possible. Once past the goal line, the offensive players are safe and can stop running. At the conclusion of the play, the instructor gets a tally of the number of flags pulled. The teams reverse roles and play again. The objective is to pull a higher number of flags than the opponents.

Ultimate Football

This fun game is actually an adaptation of Ultimate Frisbee (see page 94). With cones, mark off a rectangular-shaped field approximately 60 feet by 100 feet in size. Form two equal teams of five to ten players. Designate one team to start on offense with the football at the center of the field.

The objective is to score a touchdown by catching a pass past the opponent's goal line. There are no set positions, but the player with the football starts in the middle of the field and begins with a pass to a teammate. Players in possession of the football are not allowed to run or walk with it. Instead, the ball can only be advanced down the field by a combination of completed passes. In addition, passers have only up to five seconds to pass the ball. A violation of taking too long to pass, or walking/running with the ball, results in the opposing team gaining possession of the ball at that spot.

As long as a team successfully catches the ball, they are entitled to an unlimited number of plays. However, an incomplete pass results in the other team taking possession of the ball at that spot. Also, a pass can be intercepted by a defender which results in a change of possession. At all times, defensive players must stay at least three feet from offensive players.

A touchdown (worth six points) is scored each time a receiver catches a pass past the opponent's goal line. After each touchdown, the non-scoring team starts at midfield with the football.

Soccer

INTRODUCTION

Soccer is the most widely played organized sport in the world. Its popularity among children is due, in part, to the fact that they can play at very early age and enjoy success. The many advantages of including this sport in the recess curriculum include the high level of healthy movement required for play, its limited expenses, the potential for participation by groups of any size, and the easy-to-understand rules.

NUMBER OF PLAYERS

Two teams of eleven players each

EQUIPMENT

A soccer ball, two goals, vests

HOW TO PLAY

Regulation soccer is usually played on fields that are 100-130 yards long and 50-100 yards wide. However, most elementary schools are going to have outdoor soccer fields that are much smaller in size.

Soccer is a running and kicking game in which the ball is usually controlled by the feet. The game is played by two opposing teams of eleven players. A team is composed of five forwards who advance the ball and try to score; three halfbacks who move with the ball and play both offense and defense; two fullbacks who play defense; and one goalie who prevents the ball from going into the goal.

The object of the game is to gain possession of the ball, to advance it into a scoring position by passing or dribbling, and to shoot and make a score by sending the ball through the opponent's goal. The team that does not have possession of the ball attempts to stop its opponents from scoring and to secure possession of the ball itself in order to score at the other end of the field.

At the start of the game, the selection of the goals or choice of kicking-off is decided. The kick-off is used at the start of the game and after a goal has been scored. On the kick-off, the center forward on the offensive team kicks the ball from the center circle toward a teammate. The ball must travel forward at least one yard, and the kicker can not touch it again until another player has kicked it. The opposition must remain outside the circle until the ball is touched; then, players on both teams may cross the center line and play the ball.

During play, players must advance the ball with their feet, legs, torso, and head. If the ball touches a player's hand or arm from the fingertips to the shoulder, a foul is called which results in a direct free kick for the opponents.

Goalies are allowed to touch the ball only when inside the penalty box area. If they touch the ball with their hands or arms outside this box, or take more than four steps with the ball before getting rid of it, the other team is awarded with a direct free kick.

If the ball out of bounds on the sideline, it is put into play with a throw-in from the spot where it crossed the line. When making the throw-in, the thrower must have both feet in contact with the ground, and the ball must be thrown from over the head with both hands. The opponents must be at least 10 yards away from the thrower at the time of the throw-in.

When an offensive player causes the ball to go out of bounds on the end line, the defenders are awarded a goal kick. A goal kick is taken within the goal area by either the goalie or a fullback.

When a defensive player causes the ball to go out of bounds on the line, the offensive team is awarded a corner kick. The ball is placed one yard from the corner of the field and kicked into play.

An offsides infraction is called when an offensive player is closer to the opponent's goal than to the ball at a time when the ball is played in a forward direction toward that goal. In general, players may not stay at the opponent's goal and wait for the ball to be passed to them. Exceptions to this rule exist when two opponents are nearer their goal line than the offensive player at the time the ball is played, or when the ball is received directly from a throw-in, goal kick, or a corner kick.

A direct free kick, from which a goal can be scored, is awarded after a personal foul and is taken at the point of the foul. Personal fouls usually involve acts of unnecessary roughness such as tripping, pushing, holding, kicking a player, and charging another player. It is also considered a foul for a player to handle the ball with the hands or arms (except the goalie when inside the penalty area).

A penalty kick is awarded when a foul is committed in the penalty area by the defensive team. The offensive team takes the penalty kick from the penalty mark with all the players except the goalie staying outside the penalty area.

An indirect free kick, taken from the spot of the infraction, is awarded for offsides, obstruction, dangerous play such as high kicking, and other technical infractions. Unlike a direct free kick, a goal can not be scored until the ball is played or touched by another player on either team.

One point is awarded for each goal. After a goal, the team that was scored against kicks-off to restart the game.

VARIATIONS

The following soccer-type games are alternatives to the regular game. All are develop- mentally appropriate for elementary-age children and will provide lots of fun.

Modified Elementary Soccer —————

This modified version of regular soccer requires fewer players, and is played on a field that is about half the size of a regulation field. If goals aren't available, substitute two cones at each end. Divide the players into two teams of six players. The players position themselves on their half of the field (1 goalie, 2 halfbacks, and 3 forwards). After the kickoff, the forwards mainly play in the front half of the field and the halfbacks play on the defensive end. However, neither position is restricted to those areas and, on occasion, any may cross the center line.

As in regular soccer, the object of the game is for players to advance the ball (with their feet, legs, torso, and head) down the field and score a goal. When a goal is scored, the ball goes back to the center and the non-scoring team kicks off to restart the game.

Four Ball Shootout

Four Ball Shootout is a fun game that requires far more movement than the regular soccer. It's played on a regulation size field, but there are no boundary lines (just the two goals). Form two equal teams of eight to eleven players each. A goalie is positioned in front of the goals. The other players do not have set positions, but do need to start the game on their own side of the field for the kickoff. Place four soccer balls in the middle of the field.

The game begins with each team trying to gain possession of the balls, advancing them down the field using legal soccer skills, and score at the opponent's goal. Because there are no set positions, players are free to roam the field after the kickoff. Regulation soccer rules apply to ball handling, fouls, etc.

Because there are no boundary lines, the ball is always in play. However, a player can only score from inside the regular boundaries of the soccer field. After each score, the player making the goal retrieves the ball, brings it back to the center of the field, and immediately kicks off. At the same time, the other balls continue to be played. Each team keeps track of their score.

Circle Soccer

Circle Soccer does not require a regular soccer field, and the easy-to-understand rules make it ideal for most grade levels. Form two teams of equal size (five to seven players on each team). Each team stands in a semicircle (with both teams now forming a circle). One player starts with the soccer ball. The object is to score by kicking the ball out of the circle below the shoulder level of players on the other team. On a signal, the player with the ball passes to a teammate or tries kicking toward the opponents for a score. The ball is kicked and passed around the circle until a score is made. Players should trap the ball before kicking, and no hands or arm contact with the ball is allowed. If the ball comes to a stop inside the circle, designate a player to get the ball, dribble it back to his or her spot, and kick to restart the game.

One point is scored each time a team kicks the ball past the opponents (below shoulder height). However, the point is awarded to the opponents if the kicked ball travels outside the circle higher than shoulder level. At the end, the team with the highest number of points wins.

Four Team Soccer

This unique game calls for the use of two balls (with a four team format), and is a nice "change up" to regular soccer. Form four equal teams of 4-6 players each. Distribute different colored vests to each team. Place two teams on each side of the field. Each team has one goalie (for a total of two goalies at each goal). The rest of the players do not have set positions, but do need to start the game on their side of the field for the kickoff.

Basically, Four Team Soccer pits four teams trying to outscore each other. Starting with the kickoff, all four teams try to gain possession of one or both balls, move it down the field using legal soccer skills, and score at their designated goal. Because there are no set positions (other than goalie), players are free to roam the entire field after the kickoff.

52

After each score, the player making the goal retrieves the ball, brings it back to the center of the field, and immediately kicks off (the other ball continues to be played).

As in regular soccer, fouls and infractions result in indirect and direct free kicks. However, this only applies only for the one ball used in the infraction; the other ball continues to be played. Each team keeps a running total of their goals made.

Soccer Pirates ────────────────────

The skills of dribbling and ball control are enhanced in this simple but fun soccer game. One soccer ball is required for each player. With traffic cones, mark off a play area that is about 50' by 50' in size (this can vary depending on the number of participants. Designate several players to begin as the "Pirates." The Pirates stand without a soccer ball opposite the other players (the "dribblers") who begin with a foot on top of their ball.

The objective is play for as long as possible without becoming a Pirate. On a signal, the Pirates chase the dribblers and attempt to steal their soccer balls using only the feet. A dribbler becomes a Pirate once he or she has the ball stolen. A new Pirate can not steal the ball from the same player who just stole his. Play continues in this fashion for two minutes.

Dribblers must use legal dribbling techniques throughout the game.

Soccer Duel ────────────────────

This easy-to-understand game calls for only two participants and does not require a regular soccer field. The play area consists of two cones placed approximately 30 feet to 50 feet apart. There are no boundary lines. The two players start by facing each other in the middle of the two cones, with one player ready to kickoff (which is actually a dribble start because there is no teammate to pass to).

The objective is to advance the ball toward the opponent's cone in order to kick and hit it for a score. If successful, one point is scored and the ball is brought back to the middle for a kickoff by the non-scoring player. After the kickoff, the player without the ball can attempt to steal the ball at anytime to become the offensive player. As in regular soccer, no player can touch the ball with his or her hands. A penalty results in the opposing player gaining possession of the ball at the spot of the infraction.

Since there are no boundary lines, a player can kick and hit the opponent's cone from any angle. At the end of play, the player with the highest number of points wins.

Soccer Doubles

For developmental learning purposes, this game is a natural progression of Soccer Duel (see previous game). Because there are now two players on a team, the "team" concept of soccer is now introduced.

As in Soccer Duel, the play area consists of two cones (the "goals") placed about 40 feet apart. There are no set positions. Designate one team to start with the kickoff in the middle of the play area.

The game is very similar to Soccer Duel except now there two players on each team. The objective is to control the ball, advance it toward the opponent's cone, and hit the cone with the ball for a score. If successful, one point is scored and the ball is brought back to the middle for a kickoff by the non-scoring team. After each kickoff, defensive players may attempt to steal the ball at anytime to gain possession. Since there are no boundary lines, players can shoot and kick an opponent's cone from any angle.

Soccer Tunnel Tag

This game is an exciting mixture of soccer and tag. One soccer ball is required for each player. With traffic cones, mark off a play area that is about 50' by 50' in size (this can vary depending on the number of of participants. Designate several players to begin as the taggers. The taggers, each holding a soccer ball, stand opposite the other players (the "dribblers") who begin with a foot on top of their ball.

The objective is to last as long as possible without getting tagged. On a signal, the taggers run after the dribblers and attempt to throw and hit their soccer balls. Once "tagged," a dribbler must stop and stand in a straddle position with the ball held above the head. A tagged player is free once a dribbler kicks a ball through his or her legs. Throughout, the game, dribblers must use legal dribbling techniques.

Softball

INTRODUCTION
Although the description below contains mostly regulation softball rules and strategies, the game can be easily modified to meet the ability levels of your students. The softball-type games that follow this main description are fun alternatives and enhance the skills of throwing, catching, and batting.

NUMBER OF PLAYERS
Two equal teams of 9 or 10 players

EQUIPMENT
One softball, four bases, one bat, gloves

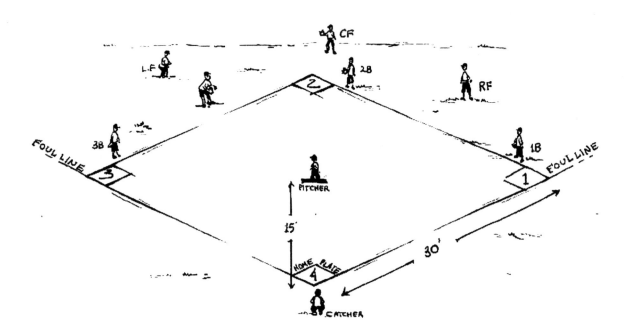

HOW TO PLAY
The official softball diamond has 60-foot baselines and a 46-foot pitching distance (for elementary-age children, these distances can be adjusted smaller). There are two teams of nine players each. The fielding positions consist of a catcher, pitcher, first baseman, second baseman, shortstop, third baseman, right fielder, center fielder, and left fielder. Slow pitch softball utilizes a tenth player called a rover or short fielder.

There are two types of softball: fast pitch and slow pitch. For elementary recess purposes, slow pitch softball is recommended. In slow pitch, the ball is pitched in a high underhanded slow arc making it easy to hit. The pitch must have an arc of 1 foot, and must not rise over 10 feet from the ground.

The game begins with the first batter attempting to hit a pitched ball, which at any time he or she can choose to swing or let it go by. If the batter swings and misses a pitched ball, it is a "strike." A batter

56

who does not swing but lets a pitched ball be thrown over the plate, between the knees and shoulder, receives a strike. A ball into foul territory is also called a strike unless the batter already has two strikes. A pitched ball that goes outside the strike zone is called a "ball." Each batter gets four balls and three strikes. After three strikes, a batter is called out. After four balls, the batter receives a "walk" which allows him/her to go to first base. A batter also receives a free pass to first base if hit by a pitched ball. If the batter hits a fair ball, he or she runs to first base, second base, third base, and home while the fielding team tries to put him or her out. The base runner may stop at any base, and continue to run the next time the ball is hit by a teammate.

A batter is called out when any of the following occurs:
- Three strikes are called
- Bunts a foul ball on the third strike
- Is tagged or called out at first base
- Hits a fair or foul fly ball that is caught
- Throws his bat more than 10 feet

A base runner can overrun first base without getting out as long as turns away from fair territory. Runners are not allowed to "lead off" (that is, the runner must have one foot on the base until the ball leaves the pitcher's hand), but may steal a base. Runners may advance to the next base on a fair hit that is not caught on the fly; however, they can advance on a caught fly ball if they wait until the ball is caught with a foot on the base (called "tagging up"). On a foul ball, runners can return to their base without being put out.

A base runner is called out when any of the following occurs:
- Touches a base that is already occupied by another base runner.
- Fails to touch a base and a fielder tags him before he can return.
- Passes another runner.
- Is tagged by a fielder when not on a base.
- Is hit by a batted ball when running off base.
- Is "forced" out; that is, the runner has to run to the next base, but the fielder with the ball touches that base first.
- Does not "tag up" on a fly hit and the fielder tags him or the base.
- Illegally leaves a base before the ball leaves the pitcher's hand.
- Runs outside the baseline in an attempt to avoid being tagged.

One point (called a "run") is scored each time a runner safely completes a run around the diamond, touching first, second, third, and home bases before three outs are made. No run is scored if the third out is a forced out, even if the runner touches home plate before the out.

The batting team switches with the fielding team after three outs. An inning is complete when both teams have had a chance to bat. A game is either seven or nine innings long.

VARIATIONS
Other softball-type games that are appropriate for the elementary school recess include the following:

Everyone Bats ─────────────────────────────

As the name of the game implies, every player on the batting team is allowed to bat despite the number of outs. The game is played using a regular softball field. Form two equal teams of nine to ten players. Have one team start in regular fielding positions and the other team to bat.

The game is played with regular softball rules with the following exceptions:
- Teams do not switch until every player on the batting team has batted.
- The last batter must circle the bases without stopping to score a run. Fielders are allowed to get the last batter out by tagging any base, including home base, ahead of the runner.
- After three outs, the batting team must clear the bases of any runners. However, as mentioned, the batting team continues batting until the last player is done.

No Outs Softball

Because there are no outs, this unique game provides lots of healthy movement. No Outs Softball is played on a regular softball field with two equal teams of six to 10 players.

One team is at bat and the other team takes regular fielding positions. The batter's objective is to hit a pitched ball into fair territory and run the bases, without stopping, until the catcher gains possession of the ball and yells 'freeze." This is the signal for the base runner to stop running and to stay in that position even if he or she is not on a base. When the next batter hits the ball, the runners start running again around the bases until the next freeze signal. Each time a base runner touches home base, his or her team is awarded one run. However, the base runners do not stop circling the bases. They continue to run and score until everyone on their team has batted. In addition, base runners may pass teammates when circling the bases. Teams switch places when the last player on the batting team has hit and stopped running on the freeze signal.

As a safety precaution, do not allow the base runners to freeze on or near home base. Instead, position the runners to the side and back of home base before the next batter starts swinging.

No Team Softball

In this fun game, there are no regular teams. Instead, every player is his or her own "team" with the goal of outscoring all the other players. Using a regular softball field, assign nine players to fielding positions with the remaining players lined up to bat.

The game is played much like regular softball except following each "out," the players rotate positions. The batter/base runner who is called out goes to right field. The right fielder moves to center field, center field to left field, left field to third base, third base to shortstop, shortstop to second base, second base to first base, first base to pitcher, pitcher to catcher, catcher to batting.

A batter continues to bat and run the bases as long as he or she is not put out. Players keep track of their own score. The objective is to end the game with the greatest number of runs.

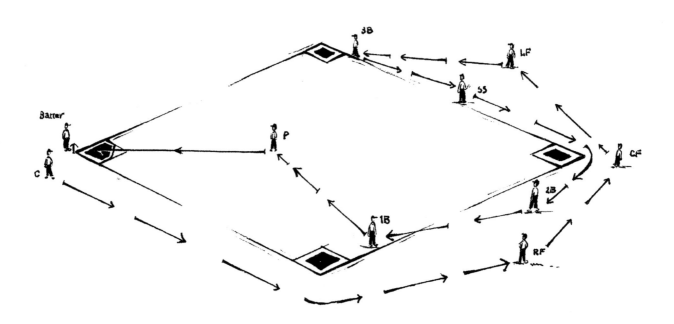

One Pitch Softball

Because the batter is allowed only one swing at the ball, this game speeds up the game of softball and adds more excitement. Assign one team to fielding positions and the other team to stand behind the backstop in a batting order.

One Pitch Softball is played much like regular softball with the following exceptions:

- The batter is allowed only one pitch. He or she must hit a fair ball or else an "out" is called.
- No bunting is allowed.
- No base stealing is allowed.
- The pitcher is a player from the batting team. This encourages accurate, easy-to-hit pitches made to the batter. The pitcher does not participate in fielding hit balls.
- Each team stays at bat until every player has batted.

Scoring follows regular softball rules.

Snake Softball

Snake Softball is a modified softball game that requires lots of healthy running! Assign one team to take regular fielding positions, and the other team to line up in a batting order behind the backstop.

The game is played with regular softball rules with the following exceptions:

- After the batter hits a fair ball, everyone on the batting team immediately forms a single file behind the batter, puts their hands on the waist of the player in front, and runs the bases as a connected unit.
- The fielding team must field the ball and throw it in the following sequence: fielder to pitcher, then to catcher, first base, second base, third base, shortstop, left field, center field, and lastly, to right field. If the batting team gets everyone across home base before the ball is thrown to everyone on the fielding team, one point is scored. However, the batting team is "out" if the fielding throws the ball to everyone in the correct sequence before the batting team crosses home base.

As in regular softball, switch batting and fielding teams after three outs.

Three Team Softball

Three Team Softball speeds up the game of softball and allows each player to experience a variety of fielding positions. A regular softball field is used. Form three equal teams of four to five players each. One team lines up to bat, one team takes infield positions (catcher, pitcher, first baseman, second baseman, and third baseman), and the third team plays outfield positions (right fielder, center fielder, left fielder, and two rovers).

The rules of regular softball apply, with the following exceptions:
- After three outs, the teams rotate, with the batters going to the outfield, the outfielders moving into the infield positions, and the infielders becoming the next batting team.
- An inning is over when all three teams have batted.

The objective is to be the team with the highest number of runs after a predetermined number of innings.

Softball 500

Softball 500 adds fun and competition to the catching of fly and ground balls. A regular softball field is not required but a large open area is needed. Since only 4-5 players can play at one time, set up multiple play areas for larger-size groups. Each game will require one bat and ball (gloves are optional).

The batter starts at one end of the field and the other players ("fielders") are spaced randomly at the other end. The batter begins by hitting a self-tossed ball toward the fielders. The fielders attempt to catch the batted ball without error for individual points. A successful catch earns the following points:
- Fly ball = 100 points
- One bounce = 75 points
- Two bounces = 50 points
- Three or more bounces = 25 points

Using the point scale, a player can also receive "minus" points for making errors. As a consequence, each player will be adding and subtracting to his or her point total throughout the game. The first fielder to receive 500 or more points will trade places with the batter and begin a new game.

Volleyball

INTRODUCTION
The game of volleyball can be played outside on a grassy area with portable nets, on a sand-based court, or indoors. Below is a description to the regulation rules of volleyball, as well as game alternatives which are fun, skill-based, and appropriate for the elementary school recess.

NUMBER OF PLAYERS
Two teams of six players each

EQUIPMENT
One volleyball and volleyball net

HOW TO PLAY
Officially, volleyball is played by two teams of six players. The three players along the net are front-row players and are called front left, front center, and front right. The other three are back-row players called back left, back center, and back right.

The team objective is to send the ball over the net so that the opposing team cannot return the ball and, at the same time, prevent the ball from hitting the ground in their court. The ball is put into play with a serve that is hit by the server over the net to the opponent's side. Before serving, the server must have both feet behind the end line on the right-hand side, and he cannot step on the line during the serve. Official rules allow the server only one chance to get the ball completely over the net and into the opponent's court. Also, the serve is lost if the ball touches the net (a net ball) and lands into the correct court. The receiving team attempts to return the served ball and a volley back and forth ensues until the ball lands on a team's own court, goes out of bounds, or is not returned properly. Each team has up to three volleys to return the ball over the net. During a volley, a player may not hit the ball twice in succession.

When the serving team wins a volley, it is awarded one point and continues to serve. When the receiving team wins a volley, it gains the right to serve (a "side out"), and the players rotate one position clockwise. Only the serving team can score. After a team has lost its serve, the team receiving the ball for the serve must rotate one position clockwise before serving.

The lines bounding the court are considered to be in bounds (that is, balls landing on the lines are counted as good. Any ball that touches or is touched by a player is considered to be inbounds, even if the player who touched the ball was outside the boundary lines. A ball going into the net can be played provided no one touches the net.

The following fouls and violations result in loss of the point or serve:
- The server fails to make a good serve.
- A player touches the ball twice in succession.
- Touching the net with any part of the body during play.
- Reaching over the net during play.
- Stepping over the centerline underneath the net.
- Holding or throwing the ball instead of clearly batting the ball.
- Letting the ball touch any part of the body other than the hands or forearms.
- Hitting the ball out of bounds.
- Allowing the ball to hit the floor on a team's own court.

The first team to reach 15 points wins the game provided they are at least 2 points ahead. If not, play continues until one team has least a 2-point advantage. A match consists of two out of three games. Teams switch courts after each game.

VARIATIONS

For elementary age children, the rules can be modified to make the game more enjoyable and to ensure a higher level of success. The following are modifications that instructors might want to consider:
- Allow the server to serve from anywhere on the court (instead of behind the end line).
- Allow the server to have two chances at making a good serve.
- Allow players an unlimited number of volleys to get the ball over the net.
- Allow players to hit the ball to themselves more than one time.

The following are volleyball-type games that are alternatives to the regulation version:

Big Ball Volleyball

This game requires a beach ball instead of a regulation volleyball. Because the beach ball is bigger and moves through the air more slowly, it's a great adaptation for elementary-age children.

Place two teams of six players on each side of the net. Designate one team to serve first. The objective is to hit the ball over the net so that it strikes the floor within the opponent's court, and to return any ball hit back by the opponents. Regular volleyball rules are observed. The first team to reach 15 points, with at least a 2-point advantage, wins the game.

Catch & Throw Volleyball

This modified volleyball game allows children to experience success early, and it allows them to learn player positioning, strategies, teamwork, and many of the rules without the stress of performing the more difficult striking and serving skills.

Catch & Throw Volleyball is played on a regular volleyball court (outdoors or indoors). Place a team of six players on each side of the net. Designate one team to serve first.

The object of the game is to throw the ball over the net so that it strikes the floor within the opponent's court, and to catch and return any ball thrown back by the opponents. The game begins with a serve (a throw) by the back-right player who is allowed to move forward toward the net if needed. The receiving team attempts to catch the ball and can either throw it to a teammate or back over the net. A team is allowed three passes before it has to over the net. After making a catch, a player must throw from that spot (that is, no walking with the ball is allowed), and has only three seconds to throw.

The serving team scores a point if the receiving team fails to return the serve or if the receiving team throws the ball out of bounds. Only the serving team can score points. However, the receiving team gets "side out" (a chance to serve) if the server fails to throw the ball over the net into their court, when the serving team allows a thrown ball to hit the floor on their side, or when a member of the serving team throws the ball out of bounds. As in regular volleyball, a team has its players rotate one position clockwise each time it wins the opportunity to serve.

Keep It Up

This easy-to-understand game develops striking skills, and doesn't require a net or court. Form groups of four to six players. Have the players in each group stand a few feet apart in a circle. One player in each group begins with a volleyball.

The player with the ball begins by making a high pass (using an overhead hit or forearm bump) to another player in the circle. The players attempt to keep the ball in play as long as possible without letting it land on the floor, or committing an illegal hit (such as carrying the ball, catching, double hitting, or letting the ball contact a body part other than the hands and arms). Each contact with the ball counts as one point. The players keep track of their score by collectively counting out loud the number of consecutive hits. The players start counting at zero again after each error. The objective is to have a higher number of consecutive hits than the other groups.

Three Team Volleyball

As the game title suggests, this is regular volleyball played with three teams. Since it requires more than the traditional twelve players (that is, six players on each team) it's an excellent game choice for large-sized groups.

The game is played on a regular volleyball court. One team of six players starts on the side of the net designated as the "serving" side. A second team of six players is positioned on the "receiving" court. A third team of six players waits to play off to the side of the court.

The objective is to stay on the "serving" side of the court longer than the other teams. The game is played with regulation volleyball rules except teams rotate places on each error or violation. If the serving team wins the point, they stay and the receiving team switches with the sideline team. If the serving team commits an error, they go off the court to the sideline, the receiving team moves to the serving side, and the waiting team moves to the receiving court. The team waiting to play always enters on the receiving side.

One point is awarded to the serving team each time the opponents commit an error or violation. At the end of play, the team with the highest number of points wins.

Four Square Volleyball

This game adds a new and challenging twist to volleyball. Four teams compete against each other at the same time with Four-Square scoring rules.

One volleyball, a volleyball standard, and four nets are needed. The nets are attached to the volleyball standard and extend straight outward (looking like a giant Four-Square court). Assign 3-6 players to each of the four courts. Designate one court as the "A" court. The team inside this court serves first. Designate the other courts as "B," "C," and "D."

The objective is to hit the volleyball over the nets so that it strikes within any of the three opposing courts, and to return any ball hit back by any of the three opposing teams. Whenever a team makes an error, it moves down to court "D."

The game begins with a serve from a player in court "A" into any of the other three courts. Play proceeds with each team attempting to return any ball into any of the other courts. A team commits an error by not returning the ball over the net by the third volley, hitting the ball out of bounds, or not making a legal serve. The team committing the error immediately moves to court "D," and the other teams move up a court. As in Four-Square, the goal is to reach the "A" court and remain there as long as possible.

LARGE GROUP GAMES

Managing a large group of children on the playground can present many challenges for the school recess professional. This section contains a variety of fun and meaningful games that are ideal for engaging a large number of students at one time. Besides developing movement skills, these games make a valuable contribution to the social growth of children and will help make the school recess an enjoyable experience for everyone involved.

Single Line Games

INTRODUCTION
Single Line Games get their classification because all of the participants are traveling toward the same boundary line at the same time. The configuration of the play area consists of two outside boundary lines with no other markings.

Because the instructor can simply mark off line lengths appropriate for any number of participants, these games are ideal for large groups of children.

NUMBER OF PLAYERS
Unlimited

EQUIPMENT
Refer to the specific game descriptions listed below for any equipment needed

HOW TO PLAY
All of the following games require a play area consisting of two boundary lines marked approximately 40 feet apart. For play instructions, refer to each specific game description.

Hill Dill

Select one player to be "It," and have him/her stand in the middle of the play area. The other players stand on one of the boundary lines and face the It. The game begins with the It calling out, "Hill Dill come over the hill. I'll catch you if you're standing still." The players then try to run across the play area to the opposite boundary line without getting tagged by the It. Tagged players join the It in the center area and become helpers for the next round. Repeat rounds until almost the entire group has become helpers.

Little Brown Bear

Little Brown Bear is a great game for having children practice locomotor (or traveling) movements. Select one player to stand in the middle of the play area and start play as the "Little Brown Bear." The other players line up on one of the sidelines and face the Little Brown Bear. The game begins with the Little Brown Bear calling out, "Who's afraid of the Little Brown Bear?" The other players respond with, "Not me." Little Brown Bear then replies, "Then I want you to run to the other side!" The players then must run to the other side (where they are safe) while the Little Brown Bear chases and attempts to tag them. Players who are tagged become Little Brown Bear "helpers." Helpers join the Little Brown Bear in the middle for the next round. Have the Little Brown call a different method of traveling (skipping, galloping, jumping, etc.) with each round. The Little Brown Bear, including any helpers, must travel in the same way as the fleeing players.

Martians

Choose one player to be the It (the "Martian") and have him/her stand in the middle of the play area facing the lined players (the "Earthlings"). The game begins with the Earthlings chanting, "Martian, Martian, will you take us to the stars?" (Or any color the Martian chooses to call out). The Earthlings wearing the designated color may walk safely to the opposite boundary line. At the same time, the Earthlings not wearing any clothing with that color run (or any other method of traveling) and avoid being tagged by the Martian. Tagged players join the Martian in the center area and become helpers for the next round. Repeat rounds until almost the entire group has become helpers.

Midnight

Choose one player to be the It (the "Fox") and have him/her stand in the middle of the play area facing the lined players (the "Chickens"). The game begins with Chickens calling out, "What time is it, Mr. (or Ms.) Fox?" The fox responds by saying any time, for example, "Four O'clock." The Chickens then walk toward the Fox, taking that number of steps. The Chickens continue to repeat the question until the Fox answers "Midnight!" At the time, the Fox chases the chickens back to their boundary line attempting to tag as many as possible. The tagged players join the Fox in the center area and become helpers for the next round. Repeat rounds until almost the entire group has become helpers.

Octopus

Choose one player to be the It (the "Octopus") and have him/her stand in the middle of the play area facing the lined players (the "Fish"). To begin, the Octopus calls out, "Fish, fish, swim across the ocean!" All of the Fish players then run (pretending they are swimming at the same time) across the play area to the opposite boundary line where they are safe. The Octopus attempts to tag as many of the Fish as possible. Players who are tagged must stay at the spot of the tag, and become "Tentacles" (or helpers). During remaining rounds, Tentacles may not move from the spot but when a player comes close to them, they can reach out and tag that player, who then also becomes a tentacle. Repeat rounds until almost the entire group has become Tentacles.

Pompom Pull-Away

Choose one player to be the "It." He or she stands in the middle of the play area while the other players line up on one of the boundary lines. The It begins the game by calling out, "Pompom pull away, run away, catch away!" The players then run and attempt to reach the opposite boundary line without being tagged by the It. Tagged players join the It in the center area and become helpers for the next round. Repeat rounds until only one player remains untagged.

Sharks & Minnows

This is essentially a variation of Octopus (see page 70). Choose one player to be the It (the "Shark") and have him/her stand in the middle of the play area facing the lined players (the "Minnows"). To begin, the Shark calls out, "Minnows, cross the ocean!" All of the Minnows then run (pretending they are swimming at the same time) across the play area to the opposite boundary line where they are safe. Meanwhile, the Shark attempts to tag as many of the Minnows as possible. Tagged players join the Shark in the center area and become helpers for the next round. Repeat rounds until only one Minnow remains untagged.

Sunday

Select one player to be "It," and have him/her stand in the middle of the play area. The other players stand on one of the boundary lines and face the It. The game begins with the It calling out any day of the week. However, the players can run only on "Sunday." The players then try to run across the play area to the opposite boundary line without getting tagged by the It. Tagged players join the It in the center area and become helpers for the next round. If a player starts running prematurely on any day other than Sunday, then he/she must join also the It in the middle. Repeat rounds until only one player remains untagged.

Trees

Choose one player to be the "It," and have him/her stand in the middle of the play area. The other players start on a boundary line. To begin, the It calls out, "Trees!" All of the players then run across the play area to the opposite boundary line where they are safe. At the same time, the It attempts to tag as many of the players as possible. Players who are tagged must stay at the spot of the tag and become "helpers." During remaining rounds, helpers may not move from the spot but when a player comes close to them, they can reach out and tag that player, who then also becomes a helper. Repeat rounds until only one player remains untagged.

Double Line Games

INTRODUCTION

Double Line Games get their classification because player movement is occurring from two opposing lines at the same time. The configuration of the play area consists of two outside boundary lines and two paralleling inside lines.

Because the instructor can mark off line lengths appropriate for any number of participants, these games are ideal for large groups of children.

NUMBER OF PLAYERS

Unlimited

EQUIPMENT

Refer to the specific game descriptions below for any equipment needed

HOW TO PLAY

All of the following games require a play area consisting of two boundary lines marked approximately 30 feet behind two middle parallel lines which are about 5 feet apart (see diagram below). For play instructions, refer to the specific game description.

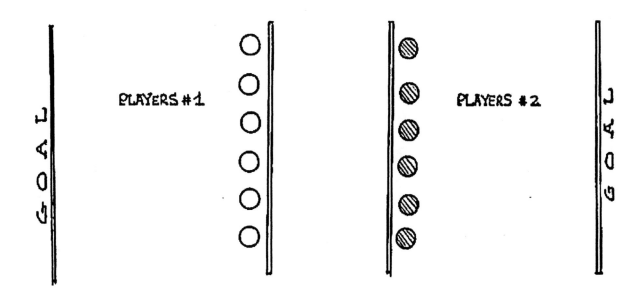

Crows & Cranes

Divide the players into two equal teams—the crows and the cranes—and have them line up facing each other on the two center lines. To begin, the game leader calls out either "Crows" or "Cranes." If "Crows" is the call, the crows will need to run to the safety line behind them and the cranes will give chase. If "Cranes" is the call, the cranes will run as quickly as possible to their safety line with the crows in pursuit. Any player tagged goes over to the other side and becomes a member of that group. After each turn, the players return to the middle and play again. At the end of a designated time the team with the most players is declared the winner.

Odds & Evens

This chasing and fleeing game, played with large foam dice (available in most P.E. supply catalogs), reinforces various mathematical skills. The two equal-sized groups stand facing each other about 5 feet part in the middle of the boundary lines. Designate one team as the "Odds" and the other as the "Evens." Before rolling the dice, the game leader announces the mathematical function to be performed. For example, "Add the two numbers together that appear on the dice when they come to a stop." The game leader then rolls the dice on the floor between the two teams. If the answer is an even number, the "Even" team chases the "Odd" team back to their safety line. If the answer comes up odd, then the "Odd" team chases the "Even" team. Any player tagged goes over to the other side and becomes a member of that group. After each turn, the groups return to the middle and play again. Other mathematical commands can include having the players subtract the smaller numbered dice from the larger numbered dice, and multiplying the two numbers displayed.

States & Capitols

States & Capitols provides an opportunity to link the learning of geography concepts with physical education. Divide the players into two equal teams—the "states" and the "capitols"—and have them line up facing each other on the two center lines. To begin, the game leader calls out either the name of a state, such as Oregon, or the name of a capitol, such as Sacramento. If a state is the call, the state players chase the capitol players toward their boundary line. If the name of a capitol is the call, the capitol players chase the state players back to their boundary line. Any player tagged goes over to the other side and becomes a member of that group. After each turn, the players return to the middle and play again. At the end of a designated time the team with the most players is declared the winner.

Truth or Consequences

This game combines the learning of various academic concepts with the fun and excitement of chasing and fleeing. The two teams stand facing each other about 5 feet part in the middle of the boundary lines. Designate one team as the "True" group and the other as "False." The game begins with the game leader calling out a statement that is unmistakably true or false. The game leader can use math problems, word spelling, geography facts, and so on. If the statement is true, the "True" players chases the "False" players back to their boundary line and attempt to tag as many as possible. Likewise, a false statement results in the "False" players chasing the "True" players. Any player tagged goes over to the other side and becomes a member of that group. After each turn, the players return to the middle and play again.

Vowels & Consonants

Vowels & Consonants provides an opportunity to link the learning of language arts with movement. Divide the players into two equal teams—the "vowels" and the "consonants"—and have them line up facing each other on the two center lines. To begin, the game leader calls out a letter. If a vowel is the call, such as "e," the vowel players chase the consonant players toward their boundary line. If the name of a consonant is the call, such as "n," the consonant players chase the vowel players back to their boundary line. Any player tagged goes over to the other side and becomes a member of that group. After each turn, the players return to the middle and play again. At the end of a designated time the team with the most players is declared the winner.

Alaskan Baseball

Grades 3-6

INTRODUCTION
This easy-to-understand outdoor game develops the skills of kicking, throwing, striking, and running.

NUMBER OF PLAYERS
Unlimited

EQUIPMENT
One ball (either a playground ball, volleyball, or soccer ball)

HOW TO PLAY
This game is played on a traditional baseball field with a home base. Organize the players into two equal teams. One team scatters around the baseball field in fair territory to play defense. The other team begins on offense and lines up in a straight line behind home base.

The first player in line (the "batter") begins the game by throwing, punting, kicking or striking the ball anywhere out into fair territory. He or she then starts to run around the line of teammates (who are standing close together in a file formation). Each time the runner circles around his or her teammates and touches home base, the team calls out a loud count. Meanwhile, the first defensive to field the ball must stand still at that spot. All of the remaining defensive players then run and line up behind the player with the ball. The ball is then passed back overhead, with each player handling the ball. When the last player has the ball, he or she yells "Stop!" At this signal, the batter must stop running and a count is recorded of the number of times the batter was able to circle his or her teammates. Any batter who ends up at least half way around his or her teammates at the time of the stop signal is credited with a point. The teams trade places after every player on the offensive team has batted.

Beanbag Robbery

INTRODUCTION
Beanbag Robbery, a variation of Capture the Flag, promotes team strategy, self-responsibility, and provides lots of healthy movement.

NUMBER OF PLAYERS
Unlimited; arrange the players into two equal-sized teams

EQUIPMENT
Twenty beanbags, two hoops, pinnies or identification vests for each team, and marking cones

HOW TO PLAY
With the cones, mark off a play area that is about 50 feet wide and 60 feet long. A center dividing line should be marked to create two equal halves. Designate the prison area on each side by utilizing two of the corners. Ten beanbags are placed inside a large hoop (the "bank") in each half.

Divide the players into two equal teams, each team lined up on their side of the center line. Each team must wear different-colored pinnies or vests for identification reasons. Each team can have one "jail guard" and one "bank guard."

On a starting signal, each team rushes for the other team's beanbags; however, players may only grab one beanbag at a time. Any player who successfully steals a beanbag places it inside the bank on his or her side. Players may be tagged and jailed by an opponent once they step across the center into enemy territory. Additionally, any player tagged while in possession of a beanbag on the opponent's side must return the beanbag to the bank and go to that team's prison. Players may free their teammates in the prisons by making it successfully into the prison, holding hands with one prisoner, and waking him or her back across the center line with hands joined.

The first team to have twenty beanbags (that is, the opponent's ten beanbags coupled with a team's own ten beanbags) is declared the winner. Since this may take a long time to happen, the instructor may choose to play with only five beanbags in each bank.

Capture the Flags

INTRODUCTION
Capture the Flags, a variation of the popular playground game called Capture the Flag, promotes team strategy, self-responsibility, and lots of healthy movement.

NUMBER OF PLAYERS
Unlimited; arrange the players into two equal-sized teams

EQUIPMENT
Three flags (or substitute similar items like scarves or handkerchiefs) for each team, two hula hoops, and cones for marking the boundaries

HOW TO PLAY
With the cones, mark off a play area that is about 50 feet wide and 60 feet long. A center dividing line should be marked to create two equal halves. Designate the prison area on each side by utilizing two of the corners. Three flags are placed inside a large hula hoop in the opposite corners.

Divide the players into two equal teams, each team lined up on their side of the center line. On a starting signal, each team rushes for the other team's flags. Any players tagged before they have a flag in hand must go to that team's prison. If a player is successful in grabbing one of the flags, he or she is safe from tagging and may walk/run it back to their own hula hoop. Players may free their teammates in the prisons by making it successfully into the prison, holding hands with one prisoner, and waking him or her back across the center line with hands joined.

The first team to have six flags (the opponent's three flags coupled with a team's own three flags) is the winner. Since this may take a long time to happen (particularly if the teams are equally matched), the instructor may choose to play with only one or two flags on each side.

Cross Country ABC'S

INTRODUCTION
This cross-disciplinary activity allows students to accomplish an academic goal and participate in a cross country jog simultaneously. Besides enhancing cardiovascular fitness, children will practice letter identification and spelling.

NUMBER OF PLAYERS
Arrange the players into pairs; an unlimited number of pairs can participate simultaneously

EQUIPMENT
Each pair of students will need a tally sheet and pencil

HOW TO PLAY
Cross Country ABC's is best done on an open playground with a measured course. Have each child pair up with another. Each pair starts with a tally sheet and shortened pencil (about 2-3 inches in length). Other than recording, the pencil cannot be held and must stay in the back pocket of one of the children.

Have the students jog slowly around the course. At the same time, they are to observe their surroundings trying to identify one item (the name of an animal, person, object, and so forth) that starts with each letter of the alphabet. For safety purposes, the students must come to a stop when recording. However, they resume jogging immediately when finished. The objective is to finish the course *and* have the tally sheet filled in with one word representing each letter of the alphabet. Allow the students to repeat the course if needed.

Cross Country Flying

INTRODUCTION
Cross Country Flying is designed to improve cardiovascular fitness by combining long distance running with the skill of frisbee throwing. Because children love to play with frisbees, this activity can make the act of running more enjoyable and challenging.

NUMBER OF PLAYERS
Unlimited

EQUIPMENT
One frisbee for each player

HOW TO PLAY
Utilizing the playground or a large field, measure out a cross country course. Have the students stand on a starting line, each holding a frisbee.

On a starting signal, each player tosses his or her frisbee, runs and picks it up, throws again, etc., until he or she has finished the course. The objective is to cover the distance in as few throws as possible (instead of keeping track of the time or places).

An alternative to throwing for distance is to have the students hit a series of targets set up around the course. Again, the objective would be to still finish the course in the fewest number of throws.

VARIATION
Consider substituting a soccer ball for a frisbee and play **Soccer Cross Country.** The game is played as described above but students dribble and kick a soccer ball.

Destination Run

INTRODUCTION
Although the chief objective of Destination Run is to enhance cardiovascular fitness, it can also be used to review general academic concepts related to geography.

NUMBER OF PLAYERS
Unlimited

EQUIPMENT
A pencil and tally sheet for each student

HOW TO PLAY
This activity is best played on the open playground with a measured course. Each student will need a tally sheet and pencil.

Destination Run can be done individually, in teams, pairs, or together as an entire group. Have the students select a destination (a nearby school, city, state) and determine the number of miles to that destination from the school. The students begin running the course, keeping track of their accumulated distance. The goal is to eventually achieve the total distance needed to reach the desired destination. This can be an ongoing activity that children can participate in over several recess periods or even longer.

VARIATION
Consider playing with one of the following variations:
    (1) Allow the students to accumulate distances during non-recess periods (that is, before school, after school, physical education class, etc.)
    (2) For added motivation, have the students play the activity in a competitive setting (that is, class versus class or pit grade levels against one another).

Garbage Ball

INTRODUCTION
Garbage Ball promotes the development of throwing skills. The easy-to-understand rules make it appropriate for a wide range of grade levels and it can be played outside or in a gymnasium.

NUMBER OF PLAYERS
Unlimited

EQUIPMENT
One foam or yarn ball for each player

HOW TO PLAY
This throwing-and-catching game calls for a play area that is about the size of a basketball court. A middle line divides the play area.

Divide the players into two equal-size teams with each team standing on their half of the play area. Each player has a small ball (for safety reasons, use only foam or yarn balls).

On a starting signal, the players begin throwing the balls across the center line into the opponent's side. At the same time, players quickly return any balls they find thrown into their side. The object is to have fewer balls in your team's area than the opponent's when the game ends. Each game can last 1-3 minutes. Allow time for several rounds of play.

VARIATION
Consider changing the type of throw used with each round. That is, use the underhand throw if the players previously used the overhand throw.

Cone Knockout

INTRODUCTION

This is a terrific game for the limited-time school recess. The easy-to-understand rules and high level of movement also makes it appropriate for a wide range of grade levels.

NUMBER OF PLAYERS

Unlimited

EQUIPMENT

18-25 cones; paper cards and tape for marking letters on the cones

HOW TO PLAY

Use a play area that is about 40 feet by 40 feet in size. Place the cones randomly throughout the play area in an upright position.

Divide the players into two even teams. Designate one team as the "Ups" and the other as the "Downs." On a starting signal, the "Downs" run around the play area and try to knock over as many cones as they can. At the same time, the "Ups" set up as many cones as they can. At the end of a designated time period (1 minute or less), the team that has more cones in their desired position (upright or knocked over) is declared the winner. Repeat the game several times.

VARIATION

Consider playing **Letter Knockout**. Mark the cones (using paper and tape) with letters that are either consonants or vowels. The game is played like Cone Knockout except the two teams would be called "Consonants" and "Vowels." The object is to have more cones standing than the other team. This is a great activity for helping children differentiate between consonants and vowels.

Foot Golf

INTRODUCTION

As in Frisbee Golf (see next game), here's a version of golf that doesn't require green fees, clubs or even balls—just a lot of imagination! Besides improving kicking skills, students learn golf strategy and etiquette.

NUMBER OF PLAYERS

4-6 players to a course; a "shotgun" approach can be used with larger groups (that is, start with 2-4 players at each hole).

EQUIPMENT

9 hoops (or substitute jump ropes), 9 numbered traffic cones, 1 soccer ball for each player

HOW TO PLAY

Set up a "golf course" by placing hoops (or substitute jump ropes laid out in a circular shape) approximately 50-70 feet apart in a scattered formation. This distance can vary depending on the age and skill level of the players. Place a numbered traffic cone inside each hoop to indicate the hole number (in all, nine holes). Assign 4-6 players to a course; add additional players at each hole if using a shotgun format. Have the players decide a kicking order.

The first player kicks a soccer ball toward hole #1, trying to land it inside the hoop. In order, the other players do the same. Golf etiquette states that the player farthest from the hole kicks first on the next round of throws. Players continue in this fashion until all have "holed out." The player with the lowest score (that is, the fewest kicks attempted to place the ball inside the hoop) is allowed to kick first for the next hole. The objective is to finish the course with the fewest number of kicks (or "strokes").

VARIATION

Instead of using hoops for the holes, consider using natural or playground objects such as trees, tetherball poles, benches, shrubs, etc. With a little imagination, the students can design their own their own "putt-putt" course.

Frisbee Golf

Grades 3-6

INTRODUCTION
Here's a version of golf that doesn't require green fees, clubs or even golf balls—just a lot of imagination! Beside frisbee throwing, students learn golf strategy and etiquette.

NUMBER OF PLAYERS
4-6 players to a course; a "shotgun" approach can be used with larger groups (that is, start with 2-4 players at each hole).

EQUIPMENT
9 hoops (or substitute jump ropes), 9 numbered traffic cones, 1 frisbee for each player

HOW TO PLAY
Set up a "golf course" by placing hoops (or substitute jump ropes laid out in a circular shape) approximately 50 feet apart in a scattered formation. This distance can vary depending on the age and skill level of the players. Place a numbered traffic cone inside each hoop to indicate the hole number (in all, nine holes). Assign 4-6 players to a course; add additional players at each hole if using a shotgun format. Have the players decide a throwing order.

  The first player throws a frisbee toward hole #1, trying to land it inside the hoop. In order, the other players do the same. Golf etiquette states that the player farthest from the hole throws first on the next round of throws. Players continue in this fashion until all have "holed out." The player with the lowest score (that is, the fewest throws attempted to place the frisbee inside the hoop) is allowed to throw first for the next hole. The objective is to finish the course with the fewest number of throws (or "strokes").

VARIATION
Instead of using hoops for the holes, consider using natural or playground objects such as trees, tetherball poles, benches, shrubs, etc. With a little imagination, the students can design their own their own "putt-putt" course.

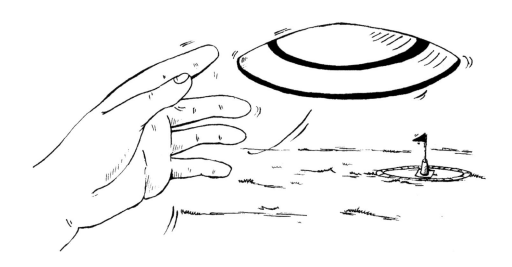

85

Number Chase

INTRODUCTION
Number Chase is a chasing and fleeing game that children in the intermediate grades will find both challenging and fun.

NUMBER OF PLAYERS
Arrange the players into individual circles of 9-12 players; an unlimited number of groups can play simultaneously

EQUIPMENT
None

HOW TO PLAY
The players start in a circle formation and are to number off by fours. After the instructor calls out a number from one to four, the players with that number will race counter-clockwise around the outside of the circle trying to get back to their spot without being tagged by any of the other circling runners (and, at the same time, trying to tag the runner ahead of him or her). The objective is both to avoid getting tagged *and* to tag others. Players can keep track of their scores. After every few rounds have the players switch places and number off again.

VARIATION
Consider having the players run two or more laps instead of one. For building endurance, consider making the circle bigger (extra spacing between the players) with each round.

Prisoner's Base

INTRODUCTION
This playground favorite actually has its origin in the ancient Olympic Games. Prisoner's Base entails running, tagging, and strategy.

NUMBER OF PLAYERS
Arrange the players into two equal-sized teams

EQUIPMENT
Chalk or cones to mark the lines and boundaries

HOW TO PLAY
Depending on the number of participants, mark off a play area that is about 50 feet long and 40 feet wide. In addition, mark off a center line and a corner in each half as "prisons."

Form two teams and send them to opposite sides of the center line. Assign one player from each team to start as a "prisoner" in the opponent's prison.

At the beginning of the game, some players should concentrate on getting to the opposite prison to free their teammate, while others remain back to defend their own prison. Players can be tagged and sent to prison once they step across the center line into enemy territory. However, a prisoner can be freed if a fellow teammate makes it into the prison without getting tagged. Both the rescuer and freed player must hold their hands high in the air when walking back to their side (if not, both can be tagged). Once a rescuer successfully makes it into a prison to rescue a teammate, he or she cannot be tagged.

The game ends when one team has captured all the opponents *or* if one team has fewer players in the opponent's prison after a designated time period.

Red Light - Green Light

INTRODUCTION

This easy-to-understand game has long been a favorite for children in the primary grades. Running, stopping, and listening are the primary skills utilized.

NUMBER OF PLAYERS

Unlimited

EQUIPMENT

None

HOW TO PLAY

Designate a starting line and finish line that are about 40-50 feet apart. Choose one player to be the traffic signal (the "caller"). The other players stand on the starting line facing the traffic signal (who is standing on the finish line).

The game begins with the traffic signal turning his or her back to the players and saying "Green Light." At this time the players run toward the traffic signal. However, at any time, the traffic signal can call out "Red Light." On this signal, the players must stop and freeze before the traffic signal turns around. If the traffic signal spots any players still moving, they must go back to the start line. The first player to make it all the way to the finish line (and tagging the traffic signal) becomes the new traffic signal.

VARIATION

Consider having the players travel in different locomotor movements other than running (that is, skipping, galloping, jumping, and so forth).

Roller Ball

INTRODUCTION
Roller Ball is a safer version of regular dodgeball. It includes rolling the ball at the feet of other players instead of the normal throwing and hitting.

NUMBER OF PLAYERS
Unlimited

EQUIPMENT
One playground ball for half of the players

HOW TO PLAY
Divide the students into two groups. Have one group form a circle; the other half spreads out inside the circle. Each circle player begins with a playground ball.

   The circle players begin play by rolling their balls at the feet of the center players, trying to touch them with the balls. The center players can move around to avoid the balls. Any center player touched by a ball must leave the center area and join the circle players. Play continues in this fashion until no one is left in the center area.

VARIATION
Consider playing the above game in a continuous non-stop fashion by having the center player hit by a ball switch positions with the roller who hit him or her.

Squirrels in the Trees

INTRODUCTION
Squirrels in the Trees promotes cooperation, decision making, and adds lots of challenging fun to the school recess. In addition, the easy-to-understand rules make it an ideal activity for children in the primary grade levels.

NUMBER OF PLAYERS
Arrange the players into groups of three players each; an unlimited number of groups can play simultaneously

EQUIPMENT
None

HOW TO PLAY
Divide the players into groups of three; two players face each other and hold hands up high to form a "tree", and the remaining player stands inside the tree as a "squirrel". One extra "squirrel" should be positioned without a tree.

On a signal, each squirrel moves out of his/her tree to an available empty tree. At the same time, the extra squirrel hurriedly attempts to find a tree. Only one squirrel is allowed in each tree and a squirrel cannot return to a tree where he/she had been previously. The objective for the squirrels is to never be the one left without a tree.

A system of rotation is necessary so that all the children have a chance at being a squirrel. For example, after a few calls, ask the squirrels to face one of the tree players. The player they are facing becomes their partner for a tree and the other player becomes a new squirrel.

Steal the Beans

INTRODUCTION
This fun team activity will keep children running for a long time!

NUMBER OF PLAYERS
The game description below calls for 16 players; however, just add additional hoops for a higher number of participants.

EQUIPMENT
15-30 beanbags; 5 hoops

HOW TO PLAY
Five hoops are arranged with one in each corner and the other in the center (see diagram above). Any distance between the hoops can be used, but 20-30 feet will be adequate for most age groups. Place an equal number of beanbags in each hoop. Divide the players into four teams and have each team stand in a line behind their designated hoop.

The object of the game is to steal beanbags from the center and outside hoops, return them to the home hoop, and have the highest number of beanbags at the end of play. On a starting signal, the first player from each team runs to the center hoop or any one of the outside hoops to "steal" a beanbag. After returning the beanbag to the home hoop, the player runs to the back of his or team line, and the next player then begins. After all the beanbags have been taken from the center hoop, players must steal from the hoops of the other teams. The following rules are to be enforced:

- A player can take only one beanbag at a time.
- Only one player from each team can be stealing at one time.
- No team can defend or protect its beanbags from being stolen.
- No throwing allowed. Beanbags must be "placed" in the hoop by each returning player.

At the end of a designated time period, the team with the most beanbags in their hoop is declared the winner. A scoring alternative is to have each team try to be the first to reach a predetermined number of beanbags.

91

Touchdown

INTRODUCTION
This game requires running, dodging, and strategy. In addition, the easy-to-understand rules make it appropriate for a wide range of grade levels.

NUMBER OF PLAYERS
Unlimited

EQUIPMENT
One small coin

HOW TO PLAY
This game calls for a play area that is about the size of a basketball court. Divide the players into two teams—the Offense and the Defense—with each team standing on opposite ends (the "goal" lines).

To begin, the offensive team huddles and the game leader designates one player to carry the coin (the "football"). Before breaking the huddle, remind all of the offensive players to close their hands so that the defensive players can't tell who has the coin. The offensive team then moves out of the huddle and spreads out along their goal line. On the signal "Hike," the offensive players run toward the opposite goal line, and the defensive players run forward and try to tag the offensive players. An offensive player who gets tagged must immediately stop running and open both hands to show whether or not he or she has the coin. A "touchdown" is scored if the player carrying the coin reaches the goal line without being tagged. The teams then reverse roles and resume play. The teams keep taking turns until time is called.

Tug-of-War

INTRODUCTION
Here's a classic large-group game that was once an Olympic event from 1900 through 1920.

NUMBER OF PLAYERS
Unlimited

EQUIPMENT
One long tug-of-war rope

HOW TO PLAY
Divide the players into two teams of equal number and size. Establish a center line in the pulling area. Tie a rag around the exact middle of the rope to mark it, and position the rope with this marker over the center line. Have each team line up single file on either side of the rope. Each player should hold on to the rope with both hands, and have three or four feet of space between each other. The strongest and biggest players can be positioned at the end of the rope to serve as anchors. On a signal, both teams attempt to pull the first member of the other team across the center line. The game ends when that player touches the line. Play several times.

Ultimate Frisbee

INTRODUCTION
This fast-action game develops frisbee skills and cardiovascular fitness.

NUMBER OF PLAYERS
Unlimited

EQUIPMENT
One frisbee, cones, different-colored vests for each team

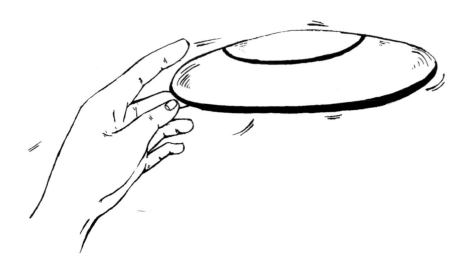

HOW TO PLAY
This game is played on a traditional football field with marked goal lines and end zones; however, the size of the play area can be modified depending on the age and number of participants. Organize the players into two equal teams. One team starts on offense and scatters around their half of the field to receive the opening throw. The other team begins on defense and lines up in a straight line along midfield. One player from the defensive team begins play by throwing the frisbee downfield toward the offensive team. The objective of the team on offense is to move the frisbee down the field and throw it into the opposing team's end zone for a score (worth one point). Offensive players cannot run with the frisbee. The only way they can move the frisbee downfield is by throwing and catching with teammates. Players may pivot on one foot while trying to find a teammate to throw to.

Defensive players may try to intercept the frisbee or knock it away in order to gain possession. However, defensive players must stay about three feet away from any offensive player who has the frisbee in her or his hands. An offensive player with possession of the frisbee has only five seconds to throw it to a teammate— or else, the disc is forfeited to the other team at that spot. In addition, any throw that is not caught (and hits the ground) results in the other team taking possession at that spot. After each score, the team that did not score is to receive a throw from the opposing team at midfield and begins on offense.

Ultimate Team Handball

INTRODUCTION
This outdoor game develops the skills of throwing and catching.

NUMBER OF PLAYERS
Unlimited

EQUIPMENT
One ball (can be a football, playground ball, volleyball, or soccer ball)

HOW TO PLAY
This game is played on a traditional soccer field (however, the size of the play area can be modified depending on the age and number of participants). The regular soccer goal posts are used for scoring. Organize the players into two equal teams. One team scatters around their half of the field to play defense. The other team begins on offense and lines up in a straight line along midfield.

   The objective of the team on offense (the team with possession of the ball) is to move the ball down the field and throw it into the opposing team's goal for a score (worth one point). Offensive players cannot run with the ball. The only way they can move the ball downfield is by throwing and catching with teammates. At the same time, defensive players may try to intercept the ball or knock it away in order to gain possession. However, defensive players must stay about three feet away from any offensive player who has the ball in her or his hands. Each player that has possession of the ball has only five seconds to throw the ball to a teammate—or else, the ball is forfeited to the other team at that spot. In addition, any throw that is not caught (and hits the ground) results in the other team taking possession at that spot.

   After each score, the team that did not score starts on offense with the ball at midfield.

Section 4

SMALL GROUP GAMES

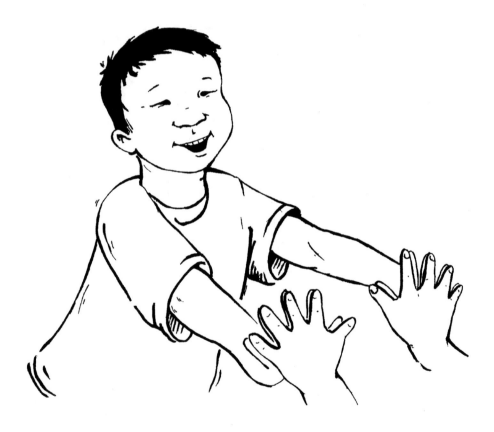

The small-group games contained in this section require only two to five participants. As a consequence, the use of small-group games maximizes individual student participation. This provides a higher level of skill development, fitness enhancement, social growth, and fun for all students. To use these activities in a recess setting, simply position children into groups of the correct size and play multiple games simultaneously.

Partner Beanbag Challenges

INTRODUCTION

The following beanbag games will provide opportunities for children to experience lots of fitness enhancement—and fun! As with one-on-one competitions (see page 101), these are ideal introductory and closing activities for the school recess. They can also be used as "time fillers" when setting up or removing equipment between the other planned recess activities.

NUMBER OF PLAYERS

Each student pairs up with a partner; unlimited pairs

EQUIPMENT

One beanbag for each pair of students

HOW TO PLAY

See the specific game described below for play instructions.

Beanbag Foot Tag

This fun partner activity enhances cardiovascular endurance and throwing skills. Each player starts with a beanbag. On a signal, each player attempts to "tag" the other by throwing the beanbag at their feet (while, at the same time, avoiding being tagged). A player is awarded one for each successful tag. The beanbag must make contact with the opponent's shoes for it to count. Play continues until one player has reached a predetermined number of points.

Push-up Steal the Bacon

Like Push-up Hockey, this game is played with the partners in a push-up position and enhances upper body strength and endurance. To begin, have the players face each other in a push-up position (with their heads about a foot apart). A beanbag is placed on the floor in the middle of the two players. On a signal, each player reacts quickly by trying to grab the beanbag before his or her partner can do so. A point is awarded to the first player who grabs the beanbag. The beanbag is placed back in the middle after each turn. If desired, the game leader can stipulate which hand is to be used each time to grab the beanbag.

Push-up Hockey

This "hockey" game develops upper body strength and endurance. The partners begin by facing each other about 5 feet apart in a push-up position (arms fully extended). One player is given a beanbag, and he or she starts by trying to quickly slide it through the opponent's arms (the "hockey goal"). The opponent can block the beanbag with an arm or hand. Players alternate turns at scoring after each attempt. One point is awarded each time a player successfully slides the beanbag through the opponent's arms. Because the beanbag needs to "slide," and cannot be thrown in the air, it's best to play this game indoors on a tile or wood floor surface.

Snatch the Beans

This game is played much like Push-up Steal the Bacon (see page 99) except now the players are facing each other in a sitting cross-legged position. A beanbag is placed on the floor between the players. On a signal, each player attempts to be the first to grab the beanbag (before the signal, each player should have both hands resting on his or her knees). Scoring is the same as in Push-up Steal the Bacon.

Partner Competitions

INTRODUCTION

One-on-one competitions are just that—challenges between two players to match strength, speed, agility, and wits with each other. Since the goal of these activities is fitness development and fun, each participant should be encouraged to focus on bettering his or her performance rather than "winning."

Because they're easy to teach and quick to set up, one-on-one competitions are ideal beginning and ending play activities for the school recess.

NUMBER OF PLAYERS

Each student pairs up with a partner; unlimited pairs

EQUIPMENT

Refer to the specific game descriptions (below) for equipment needed

HOW TO PLAY

The following instructional procedures are recommended when using one-on-one games.

- Have the students switch partners after each bout so that each has the opportunity to have more than one opponent. A system of rotation helps eliminate the possibility of one student continually dominating another. It will also provide more of a social experience for the children.

- Pair the students according to size. A popular method is to match children who are similar in height.

- Emphasize proper play procedures and safety factors before starting play.

See the specific game described below for play instructions.

Balance Wrestle ——————————————

Begin with the partners sitting and facing each other with the knees raised and feet off the floor. Their hands are placed under their thighs to help support the legs. To begin, start with the toes touching. Each "wrestler" then tries to tip the other person backwards. A player wins a round when he or she successfully tips the other player backwards (using only the toes), or causes that player to place his or her hands on the floor.

Bear Wrestling ——————————————

Mark off a circle that is about ten feet in diameter. The partners start in the middle facing each other in a "bear" position (on all fours) with a flag hanging from the back of their belt or pocket. The objective is to win the contest by pulling the opponent's flag. The game begins with the players circling and making a variety of quick movements to position themselves for a pull of the opponent's flag. Players are to stay in a bear position (that is, they are not allowed to stand up), and have to stay inside the circle at all times. No grabbing, kicking, or any form of rough play is allowed.

Bowling Pin Wrestle

Each pair of students will need one bowling pin (or substitute a cone or poly spot). The partners hold hands facing each other with the bowling pin placed between them. On a signal, each player tries cause the other person to touch the pin by pushing and pulling with their clasped hands. Play several rounds and switch partners.

Crab Wrestling

This is a great activity for developing upper body strength. The partners begin in a "crab" position with their hands and feet on the floor and the front of their bodies facing upward. On a starting signal, the players use their feet and hands in grabbing and pulling movements to force the opponent's buttocks to touch the floor. If successful, a player is awarded one point. Play continues for a specified time period. No kicking or punching is allowed.

Finger Fencing

This contest requires both strength and body control. To begin, the partners face each other standing on their right feet only. The index fingers on their right hands should be hooked together. On a signal, each player tries to push and pull the opponent off balance using only the hooked fingers. Any movement of the left supporting foot signifies a loss. After each turn, the players change the required feet and hand positions and repeat play.

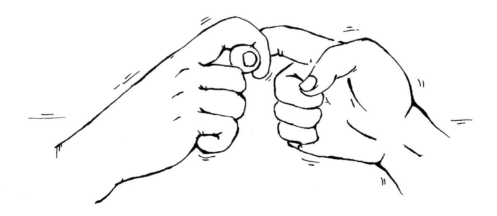

Fake & Push

The object of this game is to make your opponent lose balance without moving your own feet. Players begin by facing each other, about 2 to 3 feet apart, with the palms of both hands touching against each other and the feet together (no wide straddle stances allowed). Each player attempts to make his or her partner lose balance by pushing, dodging, or feinting. Moving a foot, no matter how slightly, signifies a loss of balance. A point is awarded to the player that is successful at causing the loss of balance. After each turn, players return to their starting positions and resume play.

Once the contest begins, the palms do not need to stay together. Moving the hands out of the way when the other player is pushing may result in the pusher's momentum carrying him or her off balance. This strategy of "feinting" is often the key to winning.

Hand Boxing

This is a fun activity for developing upper body strength. The partners start by facing each other in the up position of a push-up. Their heads should be about a foot apart. The objective is to make more "tags" on the opponent's hands than he or she is able to make. The game begins with each player attempting to tag either hand of the opponent and, at the same time, avoid being tagged on the hands by the other player. Players can use a variety of circling and feinting movements before going for a quick touch, but must remain in a push-up position throughout the contest. Each successful tag counts as one point. Play continues until one player reaches a predetermined number of points.

Hand Wrestling

Like Finger Fencing, this contest calls for strength and balance. The partners grasp right hands and place the outside edge of their right feet against each other. On a signal, each player attempts to cause the other to move either foot. This is done by pushing, pulling, and using feinting moves that cause the opponent to lose balance and, therefore, move a foot. No rough play is allowed. The objective is to cause the opponent to lose balance, not to fall down to the floor.

King of the Mountain

Mark a circle that is about 10 feet in diameter. Partners stand in a back-to-back position in the middle of the circle. On a signal, the players push backwards using only their legs. The objective is to push the opponent out of the circle. After each turn, players return to the middle and play again. Remind the players to not use their elbows and to keep their backs in contact with each other at all times.

Knee Boxing

Although punches are not thrown, the circling, feinting, and quick hand movements of this game are reminiscent of the sport of boxing. The partners begin by facing each other in a crouched position with the right hands joined. At no time during the game can a player remove his or her right hand from the grasp of the other player. On a signal, each player attempts to touch the opponent's knee (either one) with the open left hand. A player receives one point each time an opponent's knee is touched. Touching the knee with the open hand is the only kind of touch allowed. Play continues until one player has reached ten points. Players are not allowed to tackle, trip, or hang on an opponent.

Leg Wrestling

Leg Wrestling is a contest of strength and flexibility. To begin, have the partners lie side by side on their backs with their heads pointing in opposite directions. Their inside arms should be interlocked at the elbows. Both players then lift their inside leg, bend the knees slightly, and lock their legs together. At this point, each player attempts to pull the other over by pulling the locked leg down toward the ground. Repeat several times. A tumbling mat is recommended for indoor play.

Rope Wrestling

This activity is a modification of an Early American game called Rooks. To begin, place two small hula hoops about six feet apart with a player positioned inside each one. The players are then given a long jump rope (about ten feet in length), with each holding the rope so that there is an extra part of the rope (one to two feet) hanging from their hands. The object of the contest is to unbalance the opponent so that he or she steps out the hula hoop. This is done by pulling, as well as letting the rope slip a little (however, players are not allowed to totally release the rope). Remind the players that keeping one's balance during the opponent's rope slips is just as important as the strength required in the pulling part of the contest.

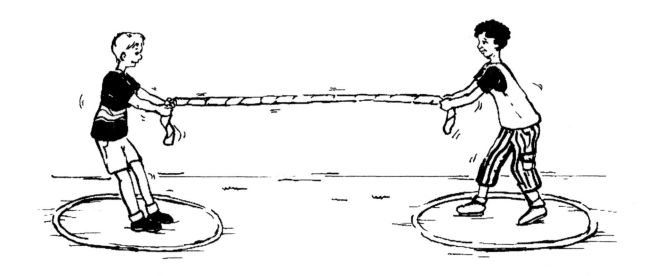

Sitting Wrestling

To begin, have the partners sit on the floor facing each other with the legs bent, feet flat on the floor, with toes touching and hands grasped. On a signal, the players pull with their grasped hands and attempt to pull the other's buttocks off the floor (scoring a point). Play for a specified time period or until one player has reached a predetermined number of points.

Toe Boxing

Like Knee Boxing, there is no punching in this game, but the circling, feinting, and quick movements of this game are reminiscent of the sport of boxing. To begin, have the players face each other with their hands placed on the shoulders of the other player. Using their feet, each player tries to touch the toes of the other player. Players can circle and make feinting movements in order to make a quick touch—however, players must keep their hands on the opponent's shoulders at all times. No kicking or stomping is allowed. Each successful "tag" counts as a point.

Partner Line Games

INTRODUCTION

The partner line games described below are basically modifications of traditional favorites such as Crows & Cranes, Steal the Bacon, etc. These changes eliminate the normal sedentary nature of those games. The result is a higher level of individual participation, movement, and fun for children.

NUMBER OF PLAYERS

Two players; unlimited pairs can play simultaneously

EQUIPMENT

Refer to the specific game descriptions (below) for equipment needed

HOW TO PLAY

All of the following games require a play area consisting of two safety lines marked approximately 30 feet behind each player. The two players start in the middle facing each other about arm's length apart.

Partner Crow & Crane ——————————————

This is a modified version of Crows & Cranes (see page 74), which is traditionally played with a larger number of children. In fact, this game is played exactly like regular Crows & Cranes except now there are only two children playing against each other (however, there can be an unlimited number of pairs playing simultaneously). The advantages here are that the game leader can better match up students according to their running abilities. And, because players aren't swerving in front of others, a safer play environment is provided.

To begin, have the partners stand facing each other about 5 feet part in the middle of the safety lines. Designate one player as the "Crow" and the other as the "Crane." When the game leader calls out "Crows," that player quickly turns and runs toward his or her safety line with the Crane in pursuit. A point is given to the Crow for successfully making it to the safety without being tagged. Likewise, a point is given to the Crane if he or she is able to tag the Crow first. After each turn, the players return to the middle and play again.

Partner Goose Chase ⎯⎯⎯⎯⎯⎯

This is a modified and more active version of Duck Duck Goose, which is traditionally played with a large group of children. The partners stand facing each other about 3 feet part in the middle of the safety lines. The players begin by taking turns tapping each other on the shoulder and saying either "Duck" or Goose." Neither player moves when "Duck" is said. However, when a player says "Goose," he or she quickly turns and runs toward the safety line while the partner gives chase. The runner wins if he or she makes it across the safety line without being tagged first. Likewise, the chaser is credited with the win if he or she tags the runner before reaching the safety line. After each turn, the players return to the middle and play again.

Partner Rock-Paper-Scissors ⎯⎯⎯⎯

This modification provides a chasing and fleeing component to the regular sedentary nature of Rock Paper Scissors. The partners stand facing each other about 3 feet part in the middle of the safety lines. The players begin by performing a rock, paper, scissors routine. A rock is a closed fist, paper is a flat hand, and scissors are the index and middle fingers in a cutting position. Paper covers rock, rock breaks scissors, and scissors cut paper. To determine a winner, the players count to three and form a rock, paper, or scissors. The winning player then chases the losing player toward his or her safety line attempting to make a tag before that player can reach the line. The chaser is awarded a point for making a tag. No points are awarded if the runner makes it back untagged to the safety line. After each turn, the players return to the middle and play again. Only the winner of the rock, paper, scissors can chase and score points.

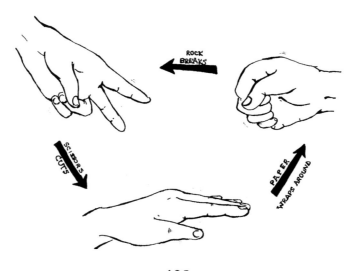

Partner Steal the Bacon

This is a modified version of Steal the Bacon, which is traditionally played with a large group of children. The partners stand facing each other about 3 feet part in the middle of the safety lines. A beanbag is placed on the floor between the players. The players begin by exchanging a handshake. This is also performed after each turn to prevent players from starting too early. After the handshake, the players are allowed to grab the beanbag at any time. The object of the game is to steal the beanbag and make it back to the safety line without getting tagged (resulting in a point), or if the other player grabs the beanbag, tagging him or her before reaching the safety line (therefore preventing a point from being scored).After each turn, the players return to the middle, place the beanbag on the ground, shake hands, and begin play again.

Partner Roll & Run

This chasing and fleeing game, played with dice, reinforces various mathematical skills. The partners stand facing each other about 3 feet part in the middle of the safety lines. Designate one player as the "odd" player and the other as "Even." Before rolling the dice, the game leader announces the mathematical function to be performed. For example, "Add the two numbers together that appear on the dice when they come to a stop." The game leader then rolls the dice on the floor between the two players. If the answer is an even number, the "Even" player chases the "Odd" player back to his or her safety line. If the answer comes up odd, then the "Odd" player chases the "Even" player. A point is awarded to the chaser who successfully tags the runner before reaching the safety line. After each turn, the players return to the middle and play again. Other mathematical commands can include having the players subtract the smaller numbered dice from the larger numbered dice, and multiplying the two numbers displayed.

Partner Truth or Consequences

This game combines the review of academic concepts with the fun and excitement of chasing and fleeing. The partners stand facing each other about 3 feet part in the middle of the safety lines. Designate one player as the "True" player and the other as "False." The game begins with the game leader calling out a statement that is unmistakably true or false. The game leader can use math problems, word spelling, geography facts, and so on. If the statement is true, the "True" player chases the "False" player back to that player's safety line and attempts to tag him or her. Likewise, a false statement results in the "False" player chasing the "True" player. A successful tag results in one point. After each turn, the players return to the middle and play again.

Catch the Fox

INTRODUCTION

Catch the Fox is played with a foxtail (a ball with a long nylon tail) which is available in most physical education catalogs. This partner game can be played as a challenge or as a team activity against other pairs of students.

This fun activity develops the skills of underhand throwing and catching.

NUMBER OF PLAYERS

Each student pairs up with a partner; unlimited pairs

EQUIPMENT

One foxtail for each pair of students

HOW TO PLAY

Have two players stand about thirty feet apart (this can vary depending on the age and/or skill level of the participants). On a starting signal, the partners begin throwing the foxtail back and forth with an underhanded throwing motion and attempt to catch it by the tail. Each successful catch by the tail is worth one point. Catching the ball itself scores no points. The two players play for a designated time and tally their accumulated points. If playing against other teams, the objective is to have the highest number of points.

VARIATION

Consider playing the partner game of Step Away (see page 117) using a foxtail. Instead of tallying points, each team attempts to end further apart than the others.

Circle Straddle Ball

INTRODUCTION

Circle Straddle Ball requires eye-hand coordination and quick reaction skills. Although it can be played with a larger number of students, it's best to keep the circles small (five participants is what is required in this game description) so students have more opportunities to handle the ball.

NUMBER OF PLAYERS

Arrange the children into groups of five players each; an unlimited number of groups can play simultaneously.

EQUIPMENT

One or more playground or soccer balls for each group

HOW TO PLAY

Place the five children in a circle formation, facing in. Each player stands in a wide straddle stance with the side of each foot touching their neighbors' feet. Their hands should be resting on their knees. One player starts with a ball.

The object of the game is to bat or roll the ball between the legs of another player before that player can get his or her hands down to stop the ball. During play, the players must catch and roll the ball rather than batting or kicking it. In addition, players must keep their hands on their knees until a ball is rolled at them. Each successful roll of the ball through another player's legs counts as one point.

After awhile, add a second ball (or third) to the game. In this case, the rollers are prime targets for other players!

Outdoor Billiards

INTRODUCTION

With a little imagination, it is possible to play billiards outdoors! Outdoor Billiards combines the strategy and rules of billiards with the skill of kicking.

NUMBER OF PLAYERS

2-4 players to a "pool table;" Set up additional play areas for large groups

EQUIPMENT

10 soccer balls, 1 playground ball, 12 traffic cones

HOW TO PLAY

Mark off a play area that is approximately 30 feet by 50 feet in size. Place two cones about 2 feet apart in the spots designated as the "pockets." Ten soccer balls are set in a tight, triangular-shaped formation at one end of the play area. A playground ball (the "cue" ball) is placed at the opposite end. Assign two players to each billiards table; partner play can allow up to four players.

The strategy is this game is much like regular Billiards. The objective is to pocket more shots than the opponent. The first player begins by kicking the cue ball toward the soccer balls, trying to knock one into a pocket (that is, the traffic cones). Any player who successfully makes a shot is allowed to keep kicking until he or she misses. After a miss, the next player begins his or her turn. If playing with two players on a team, each teammate takes turns at kicking. Play continues until one player kicks six balls into the pockets.

During play, a ball might travel outside the boundary lines. If so, take the ball and place it at the spot on the table where it went out of bounds.

Scurrying Squirrels

Grades 3-6

INTRODUCTION
Here's an active game that develops cardiovascular fitness and provides plenty of challenging fun.

NUMBER OF PLAYERS
Arrange the children in groups of four players each; an unlimited number of groups can play simultaneously.

EQUIPMENT
Five hoops, eight beanbags

HOW TO PLAY
Arrange five hoops as shown in the diagram. Any distance between the hoops can be used, but 30 feet is a challenging distance for most 3rd – 6th graders. Place the eight beanbags (the "acorns") in the middle hoop. Position a player in each of the four outside hoops.

The object of the game is to be the first player with three "acorns" resting inside his or her hoop. On a starting signal, each player runs to the middle hoop, takes one beanbag and places it inside his or her hoop. The players repeat this again until each has two beanbags. At this point, there are no beanbags left in the middle hoop and players must steal a beanbag from another player's hoop in order to achieve the goal of accumulating three "acorns." Because players cannot defend or stop beanbags from being stolen, there will always be a hoop from which to steal a beanbag. A player stealing a beanbag is allowed to take only one at a time, and must take the beanbag to his or her hoop before returning for another one. The first player to gather three acorns is declared the winner.

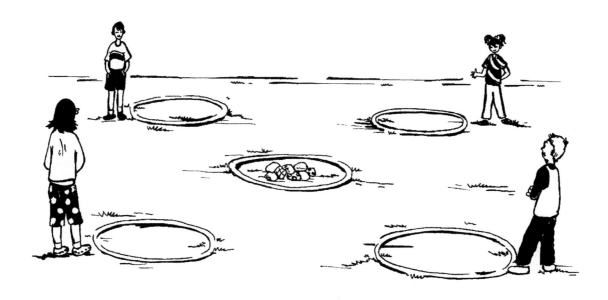

Star Juggling

INTRODUCTION

Star Juggling promotes the development of eye-hand coordination skills, and will add lots of challenging fun to the school recess! The easy-to-understand rules make it appropriate for a wide range of grade levels.

NUMBER OF PLAYERS

Arrange the players into groups of five players each; an unlimited number of groups can play simultaneously

EQUIPMENT

Up to 5 foam balls (softball-size) or beanbags per group

HOW TO PLAY

This throwing-and-catching game calls for a circle of five players. Each player stands about 4-6 feet apart from each other. Assign the players a throwing order number (see diagram below).

The game begins with player #1 throwing to player #2. Player #2 throws to player #3, and so on. After a couple of successful rounds, have player #1 start with a second ball immediately after throwing the first ball (resulting in two balls being thrown and caught). Periodically the game leader should add more balls to see how many the group can keep in play without stopping. The group's objective is to "juggle" up to five balls at one time (one ball for each player in the circle) successfully.

Caution the players to stay alert and to keep their eyes on the player throwing the ball to avoid being hit by a ball.

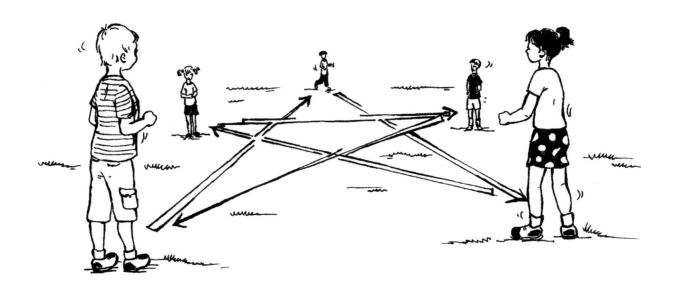

Step Away

INTRODUCTION
Step Away is a throwing-and-catching game that promotes cooperation skills and will challenge children in a wide range of grade levels.

NUMBER OF PLAYERS
Two players; additional players can play simultaneously in pairs

EQUIPMENT
A ball or beanbag for each pair of children

HOW TO PLAY
Have the two children stand facing each other about 5-6 feet apart. One player starts with a ball (or beanbag). The object of the game is to throw and catch the ball without moving the feet from the ground, and to move as far apart as possible. Each time a player successfully makes a catch without moving his feet, he or she is allowed to take one step backward. When a player fails to make a catch (or moves the feet), he or she takes a step toward the other partner. Players continue throwing and catching to see how far apart they can eventually get.

For competitive play, the couple who has moved the greatest distance apart can be declared the winners.

To provide added interest and challenge, consider changing the required type of throw or catch. Throwing can be overhand, underhand, under one leg, around the back, and so on. Catching can be two-handed, one-handed (either right or left), behind the back, and so on.

Section 5

Tag
Games

Tag games, a favorite of children around the world, have actually been around since the beginning of humankind. This section is a unique collection of tag activities that are fun and particularly relevant to elementary school recess professionals. The simple and easy-to-understand rules allow tag games to be set up quickly without lengthy periods of explanation. Further, all of these games avoid exclusionary practices—thus, maximum participation is required by everyone!

Tag Games

For most children, few games are as much fun and as easy to understand as tag. As a consequence, they also have a great deal to offer recess professionals, physical education teachers, and anyone who works with children in game settings.

Besides promoting physical activity and active participation, tag games can help develop various movement skills such as locomotion, space awareness, changing directions, traveling at various speeds, and so forth.

NUMBER OF PLAYERS
The entire classroom

EQUIPMENT
See the specific game descriptions for more information.

HOW TO PLAY
Refer to a specific game for specific play directions. The following instructional guidelines will help make the playing of tag games a more safe and exciting setting for children:

- Teaching safety awareness is important before the introduction of tag games. Because children are moving inn all directions, players need to know how to make decisions as to where to move and how to move safely. In the beginning, have the children travel with a slow jog instead of running at maximum speed.

- Use vests, pinnies, arm bands, etc., to identify the "Its."

- For large groups of children, use more than one "It." In general, a minimum of one "It" should be used with every 5-8 students.

- For tag games that are continuous, have the "Its" switch places with other students after a specified time period.

Animal Tag

A play area with two parallel lines about 40 feet apart is ideal. Divide the players into two equal groups with each group standing on a sideline. The game leader goes to one group and they quietly decide on a specific animal to imitate. The group then moves like that animal all the way over to within 5 feet or so of the watching group. The group watching now tries to guess the animal correctly. To avoid false starts and confusion, have the guessing team raise their hands to take turns at naming the animal. If they guess correctly, they chase the first group back to its line, trying to tag as many as possible. Those tagged must join the other team. The second group then selects an animal, and the roles are reversed.

Blob Tag

Select two players to hold inside hands and start as the "Blob." The other players scatter throughout the play area. The Blob chases the other players and attempts to tag them by using their outside hands. Once tagged, a player joins the Blob by holding hands. When four players make up the Blob, the Blob is divided in half, and now there are two Blobs. Each Blob continues to grow and split when they have four players. This continues until all players have been caught.

Bridge Tag

Choose one or more "Its." When an "It" tags a free player, the player must form a bridge by using their feet and hands. The tagged player must stay in this position until a free player rescues him or her by crawling under the bridge. The game is continuous and doesn't end until all the players are in a bridge position, or time has been called.

Caboose Tag

Select 3-4 players to be the "Its" (or "Cabooses"). Organize the other players into groups of 3-5 players each (the "Trains"). The players in each train stand one behind the other with their hands on the hips of the player in front of them. On the starting signal, the trains are free to run anywhere within the play area as long as they do not break apart. Each caboose (or It) attempts to catch up with a train and attach themselves to the end. When a caboose becomes attached, he or she yells out "New Caboose!" The player in front of the train immediately leaves the group and becomes the new caboose. Each new caboose has to find a different train on which to become attached. Play is continuous until time is called.

Car Tag

Select one or more players to be the "Its." On a starting signal, the "Its" chase and attempt to tag the other players (the "cars"). Once tagged, a "car" gets a flat tire and must go down on fours with one elbow collapsed on the floor. Another player can fix (and free) the broken down car by touching its head and saying "honk, honk." The car now has its flat tire fixed and is free to drive away. Play is continuous.

Cartoon Tag

Select several players to start out as "Its." On a starting signal, the "Its" chase the other players and attempt to tag as many as possible. Any player can avoid being tagged by kneeling with one on the ground and, at the same time, saying the name of a cartoon character. However, a given cartoon name can only be used once by a player.

Chain Tag

Choose one player to start as the "It." When the "It" tags one of the other players, they join inside hands and then proceed to chase others. The "chain" grows with each tagged player. The chain can not break up (that is, the tagged players must be holding hands). The game continues until all players are part of the chain.

Catch Tag

Select several players to start as "Its," and several players to start as the "throwers." Each thrower begins with a ball in their hands and, during the game, cannot be tagged. On a starting signal, the "Its" begin tagging the free players who must stand in a crouched "catching" position when tagged. However, if they catch a pass from one of the throwers, they are freed and now become a "thrower." The new thrower then looks for another frozen player to throw to. A dropped ball results in a player to remain frozen. Play is continuous until time is called.

Elbow Tag

Choose several players to be the "Its." The other players partner up and join together by locking their inside elbows. In addition, their outside hands should rest on their hips. The players must stay in this position as they move around the play area. On a starting signal, the "Its" chase and try to tag the outside elbow of any of the partners. If successful, the "It" locks elbows with the player he or she tagged and the player on the other side is now forced to let go and become an "It." Play is continuous with the "Its" being changed regularly.

Circle Tag

Divide the players into groups of four. One player in each group begins as the "It." The other players join hands to make a circle. The "It" then calls out the name of a circle player he or she will attempt to tag. The three circle players work together to avoid having the "It" tag the named player by moving clockwise or counterclockwise. The "It" can only move around the outside of the circle (that is, the "It" cannot reach across the middle of the circle). Once tagged, the player switches place with the "It." Play resumes with the new "It" calling out the name of the next player to be chased.

Everyone Is It

As the name of this game implies, everyone is an "It." On a starting signal, everyone tries to tag as many players as possible while, at the same time, avoiding being tagged. Each player keeps a running count of the number of tags he or she makes. At the end of one minute, the game leader stops the game and the players share how many tags they were able to make. The objective is to have the highest number of tags. Play several times.

First Aid Tag

Designate several players to begin as the "Its." On a starting signal, the "Its" chase the free players and attempt to tag them. Once tagged, a free player must grab that spot (where touched by the "It") with one hand but is still allowed to be chased. If that player is tagged a second time, he or she must grab that spot with the other hand but continues as a free player. When tagged a third time, the player becomes an "It." The game ends when all the players have become "Its."

Freeze Tag

Choose three players to be taggers (the "freezers") and two players (the "defrosters") to free others. The "freezers" attempt to tag all the free players while, at the same, the "defrosters" touch the frozen players and free them. Frozen players must stand with their hands on top of their hands until freed. The game can end if everyone is frozen.

Football Tag

Have the players pair up with a partner and give each pair a football. One partner starts as the "quarter-back" and the other as the "hiker." Before play begins, the game leader should demonstrate the proper technique of hiking a football. Each hiker then takes the ball and gets ready to hike the ball to the quarter-back. The quarterback, positioned about 6-8 feet behind the hiker, says "ready, set, hike." The hiker sends the ball to the quarterback on the "hike" signal. After catching the hiked ball, the quarterback then chases the hiker attempting to tag him or her with the ball (no throwing at the hiker is allowed). When the quarter-back tags the hiker, the two players change positions and begin again.

Frog Tag

Select several players to start as the "frog hunters." The other players, known as the "frogs," scatter throughout the playing area. On a starting signal, the frog hunters chase and attempt to tag as many frogs as possible. When tagged, a frog must freeze in a frog-like position (squatting, hands on the floor). Frozen frogs can be set free if a free frog leapfrogs over them. Game leaders should demonstrate how to perform the leapfrog safely before introducing this game. Play is continuous until time is called.

Germ Tag

Choose several players to start as the "Its." Before play, each "It" is given a ball (a "germ") to hold. On a starting signal, each "It" attempts to tag other players with the germ. A newly tagged player quickly takes the ball and tries to tag another player. The "Its" do not want to hold onto the germs and are not allowed to throw the ball at other players. No "touchbacks" are allowed (that is, a tagged player cannot retag the player who just tagged him or her). The game is continuous until time is called.

Got Ya

Each player begins with one beanbag. The object of the game is to "tag" others by underhand throwing the beanbag at the feet of the other players while, at the same time, avoid being tagged by others in the same manner. Players that have a beanbag hit their feet must do five jumping jacks (or any similar exercise) at that spot before rejoining the game. Play is continuous until time is called.

High Five Tag

Select several players to be the "Its." On a starting signal, the "Its" chase and attempt to tag the other players. Once tagged, a player must stand motionless with one hand held high and the palm facing outward. A tagged player can rejoin the game once a free player has "high-fived" his or her palm. Play is continuous until time is called.

Hit the Deck Tag

Select several players to be the "Its." On a starting signal, the "Its" begin chasing and tagging players. Tagged players must go down on all fours and form a bridge. A free player can release a tagged player by crawling through his or her bridge. However, a free player can "hit the deck" any time to be safe and avoid being tagged. A "hit the deck" position is lying on the back, legs and arms up in the air (and shaking). A player can stay in the "hit the deck" position for only a few seconds. Play is continuous until time is called.

Hot Pepper Tag

This tag game allows students to work on their throwing and catching skills, and requires a CD/cassette player with music. Have the students pair up with a partner, and give each pair a ball (a softball-size foam ball is ideal). The partners stand facing each other about 10-20 feet apart. When the game leader starts the music, the players throw and catch the ball back and forth. However, when the music stops, the partner with the ball chases and attempts to tag his or her partner with the ball (throwing and hitting the player is not allowed). Once tagged, the partners reverse roles and the chasing begins again. When the music starts again, the partners go back to throwing and catching.

Jumping Jack Tag

Select several players to be the "Its." Each "It" begins with a small foam ball in their hands. On a starting signal, the "Its" chase and attempt to tag the other players with the ball. Throwing and hitting another player is not allowed. Once tagged, a player takes the ball and now becomes a new "It" (the "Its" will be changing throughout the game). To avoid getting tagged, a free player can do jumping jacks at any time. The game is continuous until time is called.

Laugh Tag

Select several players to be the "Its." On a starting signal, the "Its" chase and attempt to tag the other players. Once tagged, a player must stand with hands on hips and with a sad facial expression. However, he or she can play again once a free player approaches and makes a funny face (which causes a laugh or smile). Play is continuous and doesn't end unless all the players have been tagged or time has been called.

Line Tag

This game is best played on a lined basketball court (either indoors or outdoors). Select several players to be "Its," with each holding a small foam ball. The others stand anywhere on a line. On a starting signal, the "Its" chase and attempt to tag other players with the ball. No throwing is allowed. Once a player is tagged, he or she takes the ball and becomes a new "It." All players, including the "Its," must travel on the lines. Play is continuous.

North Wind – South Wind

Start with three players chosen to be "North Wind" players (or chasers), and one or two players as the "South Wind" players (or unfreezers). Identify the north wind and south wind players with different colored vests. The north wind players chase and attempt to tag as many free players as possible. Once tagged, a player must stand motionless with hands on top of their hands (to signify that he/she needs to be rescued). The south wind players can free the tagged players by touching them on the shoulder. The north wind players are not allowed to tag the south wind player. Play is continuous.

Partner Tag

Have the players pair up and hold hands. Designate several couples to start as the "Its." Each "It" couple begins with a foam ball. On a starting signal, each of the "It" couples chase and attempt to touch the free couples with the balls. Once tagged, a couple takes the ball and becomes a new "It." No throwing is allowed. Play is continuous until time is called.

Skunk Tag

Select several players to begin as the "Its." On a starting signal, the "Its" chase and attempt to tag the other players. Once tagged, players must hold their noses and jump up and down on one foot until a free player touches them (therefore, rescuing them). An alternative method of being "frozen" would be to have players reach an arm under one knee and hold the nose. Play is continuous.

Sports Tag

Select several players to begin as the "Its." On a starting signal, the "Its" chase and attempt to tag the other players. If tagged, a player must assume a sports stance (that is, a basketball player in a shooting position, a football player in a passing position, a baseball player in a batting position, a swimmer, a soccer player in a kicking position, and so forth). A free player can rescue a tagged player by guessing the name of the sport the tagged player is trying to imitate. If the guess is incorrect, the tagged player must hold the position and wait for another player to try and guess. Play is continuous until time is called.

Squat Tag

Select several players to be the "Its," with each holding a small foam ball. On a starting signal, the "Its" chase and attempt to tag the other players with their balls. No throwing is allowed. Free players can avoid getting tagged by assuming a squatting position when they see an "It" approaching. A player that is tagged takes the ball from the "It" and becomes a new "It" (thus, the "Its" are changing throughout the game). Game leaders might want to implement a player limit of three "squats" per game to prevent overuse of the procedure.

Statue Tag

Select several players to be the "Its." On a starting signal, the "Its" chase and tag the other players. Once tagged, a player must assume the motionless position of a statue in a running position . A statue player can rejoin the game if two free players join hands around the statue and count to three out loud. Free players who are tagged while trying to release a statue must also form statues. Play ends when all the players are statues or when time is called.

Stork Tag

Select several players to be the "Its." On a starting signal, the "Its" chase and tag the other players. Once tagged, a player must assume a one-legged stork stance (one knee is held high with the foot not touching the floor; the arms are held to the side as "wings"). A tagged player is free once a free player touches his or her knee (the one being held high). Play continues until everyone is tagged or time is called.

Stuck in the Mud

Choose several players to be the "Its" and give each a foam ball. On a starting signal, the "Its" chase and attempt to tag the other players with their balls. No throwing is allowed. When tagged, a player kneels down on both knees. A free player can rescue him or her by grabbing both hands and pulling the player out of the mud. Play is continuous.

Tunnel Tag

Choose several players to be "Its." On a starting signal, the "Its" chase and attempt to tag the other players. Once tagged, a player must assume a "tunnel" position (that is, standing with feet apart, going down on all fours, an upside tunnel on all fours, and so forth). A tagged player is free once a free player crawls through his or her tunnel. Play continues until everyone is tagged or time is called.

Wall Tunnel Tag

This game is played much like Tunnel Tag (see above game). However, in this game, tagged players must go to a wall and perform a wall stand (forming a "tunnel"). This can be either a standing tunnel with the hands on a wall or a tunnel with the hands on the floor and feet on the wall. Before introducing this activity, game leaders should first teach the players how to safely perform a wall stand with the hands on the floor. Instruct the players to place their palms on the floor shoulder width apart and about 2 feet from the wall. Next, have the players slowly walk up the wall, putting their weight on their hands until their body is almost upright.

A tagged player stays in the tunnel position until he or she is rescued by having a free player crawl underneath.

RELAYS
& RACES

Relays and running games are an excellent way to challenge students and add excitement to the school recess. Relays also develop cooperative skills because they require individual participation within a group setting—that is, each student must follow specific rules to reach a common goal. This section includes relay activities for a wide range of ages and abilities. In addition, you will also find non-equipment relays and races, relays that call for specific balls, movement skill relays, and relays that utilize equipment such as hula hoops and beanbags.

Classic Relays

INTRODUCTION
In this traditional team running game (including all the variants described below), all you need is a starting/finishing line and a turning point. Besides adding the element of fun to recess play, relay races enhance cardiovascular fitness and the skill of cooperation.

NUMBER OF PLAYERS
Arrange the players into equal teams of three or four players each; an unlimited number of teams can play simultaneously

EQUIPMENT
Cone markers

HOW TO PLAY
With the cone markers, establish a starting/finishing line and a turnaround point. This distance can vary depending on the age of the participants. Divide the players into teams, with an equal number of runners on each (three or four players is ideal). Each team lines up in a file formation behind the starting/finishing line.

On a starting signal, the first runner on each team runs to his or her designated turnaround cone, circles around it, and sprints back to the starting/finishing line. The second player in line receives a tag from the finishing player and then he or she runs. Play continues in this fashion until each team has finished and all of the players are sitting in their original starting positions.

So that relay games can offer an optimal play experience at recess, the following procedures and rules are recommended.

1. Have clear direction-of-traffic rules. When runners go around the turning point, they should do it from the right (counterclockwise). In addition, runners returning to the finish line should pass by on the right side of their awaiting teammates.
2. Restrict team sizes to no more than four players. Having small team sizes increases the amount of healthy activity (that is, there is less time standing in line waiting for a turn to run).
3. Arrange the teams so that all are as equal as possible in terms of ability and skill levels. Since no team should ever have to lose more than twice in a row, try changing players on each team after each relay.
4. Rules (such as not starting early before being tagged by the returning runner) should be discussed and enforced. Relay games require children to conform to certain rules if the experience is to be enjoyable by all.

VARIATIONS
Different types of movements and challenges can be substituted for running. Here are some examples of relay games that do not require any equipment:

Bear Relay

As with all animal imitated relays, it's best to have the players practice walking like the selected animal (in this case, a bear) before starting the relay. To move like a bear, a player bends forward with both hands on the ground, and moves with the left hand and right foot forward at the same time. Then the right hand and left foot are moved forward together. As in the classic relay race, each team's players line up behind the starting line. The turning spot should be about 20 feet from the starting/finishing line. On a starting signal, the first player on each team walks like a bear to the turning spot and back to the finish line, tags the next player in line who repeats the action. This pattern continues until each player has crossed the finish line. The first team to complete the race wins.

Chariot Relay

Use cones to mark a starting/finishing line with a turning spot (about 30-40 feet apart). Form equal teams of 3-4 players. For teams with three players, have two join inside hands and stand side-by-side on the starting line. These players represent the "chariot." The third player is the driver and stands behind them, holding the outside hand of each player. For teams with four players, the same formation is made except three players hold hands to form the chariot. On a starting signal, the chariots run forward, around the turning spot, and back to the finish line. The players then quickly rotate positions with a new player as the driver, and go again. Continue the race until every player in each team has had a chance to be a driver (that is, three laps for three-player teams or four laps for four-player teams). The first team to finish wins.

Crab Relay

This relay is played exactly like the classic running relay, but now the players crawl backwards on all fours ("crab style"), beginning at the starting/finishing line. When a player reaches the turning spot, he or she continues to crab walk back to the line and tags the next "crab" who repeats the action. The first team to have all of its players return to the starting/finishing line wins the contest.

Frog Jumping Relay

This relay is played much like the classic running relay, but now the players jump like frogs, beginning at the starting line. When a player reaches the turning spot, he or she continues to frog jump back to the line and tags the next "frog" who repeats the action. The frog jump should be performed in a crouch position, knees apart, and hands placed on the ground. A player moves forward by jumping with both feet and hands together at the same time. The first team to have all of its players return to the starting/finishing line wins the contest.

Leapfrog Relay

Mark starting and finishing lines that are about 30-40 feet apart. Divide the players into equal teams of 3-4 players. Each team begins in a file formation behind the start line. On a starting signal, the player at the back of the line begins jumping over his or her teammates who are kneeled down. When the leaper reaches the end of the line, he or she becomes the front end of the line and kneels down. Then the last player in line stands up and starts jumping over the other players. This is repeated until each player has crossed the finish line. The winning team is the first to complete the task.

Man in the Moon Relay

Use cones to mark a starting/finishing line with a turning spot (about 30-40 feet apart). Form equal teams of 5-6 players. Have each team form a circle by holding hands. Designate one player in each team to stand in the middle of their circle. On a starting signal, the teams run forward, around the turning spot, and back to the finish line. The players then quickly rotate positions with a new player in the middle, and go again.

The players forming the circle must hold hands throughout the race, and they cannot touch the player in the middle. Continue the race until every player in each team has had a chance to be in the middle. The first team to finish wins.

Sedan Relay

This relay is played exactly like the Chariot Relay (see above) but the method of transportation is different. Use cones to mark a starting/finishing line with a turning spot about 30 feet apart. Form equal teams of 3 players. Each team forms a "sedan" by having two players face each other on the starting line with both hands joined. They then form a chair by lowering their front arms and moving their back arms up. The third player sits in the chair. On a starting signal, the "sedans" run forward, around the turning spot, and back to the finish line. The players then quickly rotate positions with a new player to be carried, and go again. When all the players have been carried, that team is finished. The first team to finish wins.

Rescue Relay

Use cones to mark two lines that are about 50 feet apart. Form equal teams of four players. Have each team get in a single file with one player (the "leader") standing on the opposite line facing the rest of his or her teammates. On a starting signal, the leader from each team runs forward to the first player in his or her team, grabs that person's hand and both run back to the leader's line. The leader then remains at this line while the rescued player runs back and gets another player. This continues until all of the players have been rescued. The first team to complete the task wins the relay.

Tunnel Relay

This relay is best played with separate starting and finishing lines that are about 30 feet apart. Divide the players into equal teams of 4-5 players each. The teams stand in a single file formation on the starting line with each player down in a push-up position. There should be about a foot of distance between each player. On a starting signal, the last player on each team gets on his or her knees and crawls between the legs of his or her teammates to the front of the line. Once in front, the player goes down into a push-up position. Then the next player in the back of the line goes. This rotation continues the team eventually reaches the finish line. The first team to finish wins.

Wheelbarrow Relay

Form teams of two players. The partner acting as the "wheelbarrow" goes down on his or her hands in a push-up position on the starting line. The other partner picks up the legs of the wheelbarrow. At the starting signal, the partners travel forward toward the turning spot and back with the wheelbarrow moving his or her hands as fast as possible. After arriving back to the starting/finishing line, the partners

139

exchange roles and go again. For safety purposes, remind the "drivers" to gently and slowly lower the wheelbarrow's legs when making the exchange. The first team to finish wins.

Two-Legged Relay

Form teams of four players. Have the players in each team pair up. The first partners in each team stand side-by-side and grasp each other around the waist or shoulders with the inside arm, and lift the inside foot off the ground. On a starting signal, the first pair hops to a designated turning spot and back, then the next pair goes. The first team to finish wins.

Ball Relays

INTRODUCTION
Ball relay races are played much like the classic running relay (see page 888), but now various ball-handling skills are required. In addition to enhancing cardiovascular fitness and motor skills, relays can present wonderful opportunities to teach children cooperation and sportsmanship.

NUMBER OF PLAYERS
Arrange the players into equal teams of three or four players each; an unlimited number of teams can play simultaneously

EQUIPMENT
One or more playground balls (see the specific relay described below for the required number of playground balls)

HOW TO PLAY
Refer to the specific relay described below for the set-up of the play area. Divide the players into teams, with an equal number of runners on each (three or four players is ideal). In most cases, have each team line up in a file formation behind the starting/finishing line.

Since each ball relay described below has its own play directions, please refer to a specific relay for the set-up, rules, and description. In most cases, the objective is to be the first team to successfully finish the challenge.

The following procedures and rules are recommended with all ball relays:

1. As in the classic relay race, have clear direction-of-traffic rules. If runners are required to go around a turning point, they should do it from the right (counterclockwise). In addition, runners returning to the finish line should pass by on the right side of their awaiting teammates.
2. Restrict team sizes to no more than four players. Having small team sizes increases the amount of healthy activity (that is, there is less time standing in line waiting for a turn to run).
3. Arrange the teams so that all are as equal as possible in terms of ability and skill levels. Since no team should ever have to lose more than twice in a row, try changing players on each team after each relay.
4. Rules (such as not starting early before being tagged by the returning runner) should be discussed and enforced. Relay games require children to conform to certain rules if the experience is to be enjoyable by all.

ARCH BALL RELAY ──────────────

Divide the players into equal-numbered teams. The players in each team stand in a single file formation. The player at the front of each line begins with a playground ball. On a starting signal, the first player on each team passes the ball backwards and overhead to the next player. This player continues the overhead backward passing to the next person and so on to the back player. The last player, on receiving the ball, runs to the head of the line, and the activity is repeated. This pattern continues until all the players have run and are back in their original positions. The first team to finish wins.

Over & Under Relay

This relay is played much like Arch Ball Relay (see above), but with a different twist to the required task. Divide the players into equal teams. Each team stands in a single file formation with all the players in a straddle position. The player at the front of each line begins with a playground ball. On a starting signal, the first player on each team passes the ball overhead and backwards to the next player. This player now hands the ball between his/her legs to the next player. The ball goes over and under down the line. The last player, on receiving the ball, runs to the head of the line, and the activity is repeated. This pattern continues until all the players have run and are back in their original positions. The first team to finish wins.

Straddle Ball Relay

This relay is played much like Over & Under Relay (see above), but with different twist to the required task. Divide the players into equal teams. Each team stands in a single file formation, with all the players in a straddle position. The player at the front of each line begins with a playground ball. On a starting signal, the first player on each team rolls the ball backwards (between the legs) to the last player in line. Players can help handle and roll the ball backwards. The last player, on receiving the ball, runs to the head of the line, and the activity is repeated. This pattern continues until all the players are back in their original positions. The first team to finish wins.

Tunnel Bowling Relay

Form equal teams of five to eight players, and have each team begin in a single file formation. Everyone except for the first and last person in line assumes the push-up position. The player at the head of each line begins with a playground ball. Play begins with player in front rolling the ball (as in bowling) under the other players (toward the last player), and then forming the push-up position. The last player in line receives the ball, runs to the front, rolls the ball down the line, and then forms the push-up position. This alternating pattern continues until all the players are back in their original starting positions.

Pass & Duck Relay

Form equal teams of five to eight players, and have each team stand in a single file formation. Now, position one player on each team to stand behind a line that is about 10 feet in front of his/her teammates. This player begins with a ball and facing the teammates. On a starting signal, this player passes the ball to the first player in line, who returns the ball right back with a pass, and immediately squats down. Now the next player in line receives a pass, returns it back, squats down, and this pattern continues down the line. When the last player in line receives the ball, he/she runs forward and replaces the previous head passer (who takes a place at the head of the file). The relay is over when the original passer receives the ball in the back position and returns to his/her original position.

Kangaroo Relay

Form teams of three to four players. The players begin in a single file formation behind a starting line. The first player in each team starts with a playground ball that is held by the ankles or knees. For a designated turning point, place a cone in front of each team that is about 15 feet from the starting/finishing line. On a starting signal, the first player in each team jumps (with the ball squeezed between the ankles or knees) to the turning point and back, hands the ball to the next teammate in line, and now that player begins jumping. Each player repeats the action until all have jumped. During play, if the ball falls to the ground, the player must pick it up and place it between the knees or ankles before jumping again. The first team to finish wins.

Relays with Equipment

INTRODUCTION
For the most part, relay races with equipment are played much like the classic running relay (see page 888), but now various manipulative skills are utilized because of the use of beanbags, hula hoops, and so forth. In addition to enhancing cardiovascular fitness and motor skills, relays can present wonderful opportunities to teach children cooperation and sportsmanship.

NUMBER OF PLAYERS
Arrange the players into equal teams of three or four players each; an unlimited number of teams can play simultaneously

EQUIPMENT
Cone markers, hoops, beanbags, jump ropes (see the specific relay described below for the required equipment)

HOW TO PLAY
Refer to the specific relay described below for the set-up of the play area. Divide the players into teams, with an equal number of runners on each (three or four players is ideal). In most cases, have each team line up in a file formation behind the starting/finishing line.

Since each equipment relay described below has its own play directions, please refer to a specific relay for the set-up, rules, and description. In most cases, the objective is to be the first team to successfully finish the challenge.

The following procedures and rules are recommended with all equipment relays:

1. As in the classic relay race, have clear direction-of-traffic rules. If runners are required to go around a turning point, they should do it from the right (counterclockwise). In addition, runners returning to the finish line should pass by on the right side of their awaiting teammates.
2. Restrict team sizes to no more than four players. Having small team sizes increases the amount of healthy activity (that is, there is less time standing in line waiting for a turn to run).
3. Arrange the teams so that all are as equal as possible in terms of ability and skill levels. Since no team should ever have to lose more than twice in a row, try changing players on each team after each relay.
4. Rules (such as not starting early before being tagged by the returning runner) should be discussed and enforced. Relay games require children to conform to certain rules if the experience is to be enjoyed by all.

Beanbag Carry & Catch ——————————

Divide the players into equal teams of three to four players. The players in each team stand in a single file formation behind the starting line. The player at the front of each line begins with a beanbag. Position a hula hoop in front of each team about 30 feet from the starting/finishing line. On a starting signal, the first player of each team carries the beanbag forward and puts it inside the hoop, then returns and tags the next runner. The second runner goes forward, picks up the beanbag, and runs back to the line to hand it off to the third player. Throughout the relay, one runner will carry the beanbag to the hoop and the next runner fetches it back. This pattern continues until all the players have run and are back in their original positions. The first team to finish wins.

Beanbag Hoop Exchange

This relay is played much like Beanbag Carry & Fetch (see above), but with a slightly different twist to the required task. Divide the players into equal teams of three to four players. The players in each team stand in a single file formation behind the starting line. Position two hoops in a straight line in front of each team that are about 15 and 30 feet from the starting/finishing line. Place one beanbag in the nearest hoop. On a starting signal, the first player on each team runs forward, picks up the beanbag, and moves it to the other hoop. He or she then returns back to the line and tags the next runner. The second runner goes forward, picks up the beanbag, and places it back in the other hoop. Then he or she returns and tags the next runner. Throughout the relay, one runner will carry the beanbag to one hoop and the next runner brings it back to the other hoop. This pattern continues until all the players have run and are back in their original positions, or until each has run a predetermined number of times. The first team to finish wins.

Hula Hoop Relay

This relay does not require starting/finishing lines. Form equal teams of five to eight players. The players stand side by side with hands joined. A hula hoop is placed in the free hand of the first player in each team. On a starting signal, the players move the hoop down the line so that each player passes through it. When the last player has the hoop, he or she takes it to the head of the line, and the process is repeated. Play continues until the original leader is again at the front of the line. During play, the children can manipulate the hoop with their hands as long as the hands are joined.

146

Hoop Partner Relay

Form teams of four players. Have the players in each team pair up. The first partners in each team stand side-by-side (or one partner behind the other) inside a hula hoop, which is held around their waist area with both hands. For a designated turning point, place a cone in front of each team that is about 40 feet from the starting/finishing line. On a starting signal, the first pair runs to the designated turning spot and back, hands the hoop to the next pair of teammates, and that pair repeats the action. The first team to complete the task wins.

Three Stunt Relay

Three Stunt Relay requires one short jump rope, one beanbag, one basketball, and three hula hoops for each team. Form equal teams of three to four players and have each team stand in a single-file formation behind the starting/finishing line. Three hula hoops are placed in a straight line (about 15 feet apart) in front of each team. The first hula hoop contains a beanbag, the second hoop has a jump rope, and the third contains a basketball. On a starting signal, the first player from each team runs to the first hoop, picks up the beanbag, puts it on his or her head, and balances it while moving to the next hoop. At the second hoop, he or she puts the beanbag down, picks up the jump rope, and jumps rope while running to the third hoop. There the player puts the rope down, takes the basketball, and dribbles it back to the first hula hoop. He or she puts the basketball inside the first hula hoop, runs back to his or her team, tags the next teammate, and now that player performs the tasks. The order of the tasks will be different for each player, but all will end up performing the three required tasks. Play continues in this fashion until all the players are back into their starting positions.

Hoop Rolling Relay

Prior to playing this relay, make sure that all of the players can successfully roll an upright hula hoop with their hands while running. Form teams of three to four players. The players begin in a single file formation behind the starting line. The first player in each team starts with a hula hoop. For a designated turning point, place a cone in front of each team that is about 40 feet from the starting/finishing line. On a starting signal, the first player in each team rolls an upright hula hoop continuously as he or she runs around the turning point and back, hands the hoop to the next teammate in line, and now that player begins rolling and running. Each player repeats the action until all have rolled and run. During play, if the hoop falls to the ground, the player must pick it up and start rolling again. The first team to finish wins.

Three-Legged Relay

This relay requires either a rags or scarves. Form equal teams of two players. The partners stand side by side on the starting line with their inside legs loosely tied together with a rag or scarf. For the turnaround point, place a cone in front of each team that is about 30 feet from the starting/finishing line. On a starting signal, the partners run (actually, it will be more of a "hobble") off to the turnaround point and back. The first couple back wins.

Jump Rope Relay

Prior to playing this relay, make sure that all the players can jump an individual rope while running. Form teams of three to four players. The players begin in a single file formation behind the starting line. The first player in each team starts with a jump rope. For a designated turning point, place a cone in front of each team that is about 40 feet from the starting/finishing line. On a starting signal, the first player in each team jumps the rope continuously as he or she runs around the turning point and back, hands the rope to the next teammate in line, and goes to the back of the line. Each player repeats the action until all have run. The first team to finish wins.

Train Relay

This relay requires a long jump rope for each team. Use cones to mark a starting/finishing line with a turning spot (about 30-40 feet apart) in front of each team. Form equal teams of 4-6 players. Have each team stand in a single file formation with each player grasping a long jump rope with one hand. On a starting signal, the teams run forward, around the turning spot, and back to the finish line. The players then quickly rotate positions with a new player in the front, and go again. The players cannot let go of the rope when running. Continue the race until every player in each team has had a chance to be in the front. The first team back in its original starting position wins.

Pogo Cone Relay

Standard cones (12 to 24 inches high) act as "pogo sticks" in this relay. Form equal teams of three to four players. The players begin in a single file formation behind the starting line. The first player in each team starts with his or her feet tightly squeezed around a cone. For a designated turning point, place a marker in front of each team that is about 20 feet from the starting/finishing line. On a starting signal, the first player in each team "pogo jumps" to the turning point and back, hands the cone to next teammate in line, and goes to the back of the line. Each player repeats the action until all have jumped. The first team to finish wins.

Around-the-Bases Relay

INTRODUCTION
This relay requires running around four bases that are laid out as in a softball diamond. It can also be used as a beginning or ending activity when combined with regular softball play.

NUMBER OF PLAYERS
Arrange the players into two equal teams of 3-6 players each

EQUIPMENT
Four bases

HOW TO PLAY
Divide the players into two teams, with an equal number of runners on each (3-6 players is ideal). Have each team line up in a file formation at opposite bases on the inside of the diamond.

On a starting signal, the lead-off player for each team runs around the bases in a complete circuit and is followed by each teammate in turn. When running, players must tag each base. The first team to complete the relay wins.

Cross Country Relay

INTRODUCTION

Because children naturally love to "race," this team activity can make the act of long-distance running more enjoyable and challenging. Improved fitness and cardiovascular endurance are the primary benefits of this game.

NUMBER OF PLAYERS

Unlimited teams with four players each

EQUIPMENT

One baton (or similar object) for each team, three cone markers (or substitute natural markers that are located around the playground)

HOW TO PLAY

Using a large open area, design a course with the cone markers (or substitute natural markings such as trees, playground equipment, goal posts, and so forth). Form teams of four players each. Each team decides a running order with each runner positioned at one of the four spots (see illustration). Each runner at the starting line begins with a baton (or similar object).

On a starting signal, the first runners take off toward their teammates who are positioned at the #2 spot on the course. Once there, they hand off the baton and that teammate now runs toward the next teammate positioned at spot #3. Play continues in this fashion until the last runner carries the baton across the finish line. The team objective is to complete the course as quickly as possible.

Horse & Jockey

INTRODUCTION
This running game emulates the concepts of an exciting horse race.

NUMBER OF PLAYERS
Arrange the players into pairs and assign about 6-10 pairs to a group; an unlimited number of groups can play simultaneously

EQUIPMENT
None

HOW TO PLAY
Have the players form a double circle, with those on the inside facing their partners in the outside circle (outside players should have about 3 feet distance separating each other). The players on the outside stand with their legs straddled wide apart.

On a starting signal, the inside players crawl through their partner's legs (the "starting gate") and race clockwise around the circle. After the inside player has exited through the gate, his or her partner quickly gets down on all fours (like a horse). When each runner returns to their partner, they quickly mount him or her in a jockey position. The first couple mounted as horse and jockey are declared the winners.

For safety purposes, instructors should have the players practice safe "mounting" before starting play. That is, the "jockey" should support most of his or her weight by standing in a straddle position over the "horse," not by sitting.

Pony Express

INTRODUCTION
Pony Express is a relay game which enhances cardiovascular fitness.

NUMBER OF PLAYERS
Arrange the players into teams of four players each; an unlimited number of teams can play simultaneously

EQUIPMENT
One track baton (or a similar type object) for each team, cone markers

HOW TO PLAY
Using a large open area, design an oval shape course. Place a cone marker at four stations on the course that are equally spaced apart. Form teams with four players, and assign each of the players a station to start the game. The runners at station #1 begin with batons.

On a starting signal, the runner at station #1 carries the baton to his or her teammate at station #2. After handing off the baton, the runner from station #1 stays at station #2. The runner from station #2 carries the baton to his or her teammate at station #3, hands off the baton, and stays there. The runner from station #3 carries the baton to station #4, hands off the baton, and stays there. The runner from station #4 has to carry the baton all the way (two segments) to the next teammate who is now at station #2. Throughout the game, every runner at station #4 will have to run double duty. Play continues in this fashion until all of the runners are back in their original starting positions. The objective is to be the first team to finish the race.

Total Team Relay

INTRODUCTION

This vigorous relay requires running around teammates in a circular formation. It's a great choice for developing cardiovascular fitness!

NUMBER OF PLAYERS

Arrange the players into equal teams of 5-8 players each

EQUIPMENT

None required; however, poly spots would be helpful in marking player locations

HOW TO PLAY

Divide the players into equal teams (5-8 players on each team is ideal). Have each team stand in a circular formation with a diameter of around 15 feet. The actual size of the circle can be adjusted according to the number of participants, grade level, amount of running desired, etc. If available, poly spots can be laid out to mark the placement of runners. Players will need to determine their running order before play begins.

On a starting signal, the lead-off player for each team runs around the circle in a complete circuit and is followed by each teammate in turn as he/she passes by. Each player must follow the player ahead of him/her (in other words, no "passing" is allowed). When players return to their spots they sit down. The first team to have all of its players sitting wins.

155

Rope Jumping
Activities

Rope jumping is an excellent medium for fitness development during the school recess. In addition, it requires little space, is relatively inexpensive, is suitable for both boys and girls, and most importantly–it's fun! Included in this section are teaching strategies and challenges for both long and individual rope jumping. This includes steps that are simple enough for six-year olds to master, as well as steps that are challenging even for the older and highly experienced jumper.

Long Rope Jumping

INTRODUCTION

Long rope jumping is an excellent activity for beginning jumpers, as they can concentrate on jumping the rope before learning the skill of turning. However, older children will also find long rope jumping an enjoyable experience and will be challenged in performing some of the advanced steps.

The many physical benefits of rope jumping include the development of cardiovascular endurance, strength development, agility, body control, and increased hand-eye-foot coordination. Long rope jumping also enhances social growth and group cooperation as it necessitates several players working together to accomplish a common goal.

NUMBER OF PLAYERS

Three players to a rope

EQUIPMENT

One long jump rope (10 to 12 feet long for the younger children; 14 to 16 feet long for the older children)

HOW TO PLAY

The proper execution of turning a rope is critical to successful jumping. If turning is not rhythmic, even skilled jumpers will have problems. However, turning the rope is a difficult skill for young children and it should be practiced regularly until an even, steady rhythm is developed. While the skill of turning is practiced on its own, the younger children can still participate in the non-turning jumps, such as Jump The Stick, High Water, Pendulum Jump, etc.

The following instructional procedures are essential when introducing beginning turning and jumping skills with the long ropes.

1) When teaching children how to turn, emphasize keeping the elbow close to the body and concentrate on turning the rope with the forearm. Lock the wrist and keep the thumb up while turning. The rope should barely touch the floor each time.

2) A good swing for the rope turners to use at the start of a turn is called the "blue bell" technique. That is, three pendulum swings (half swings) are followed by a full turn.

3) Beginning jumpers should concentrate on mastering the stationary jump (see Jump The Stick) and half-swing jumps (see Pendulum Jump) before attempting to jump with a full turn.

4) Introduce the terms *Front Door* and *Back Door* when children are ready to start entering a turning rope. *Front Door* means entering from the side where the rope is turning forward and toward the jumper after it reaches its peak. To enter front door, the jumper follows the rope in and jumps when it completes the turn. *Back Door* means entering from the side where the rope is turning backward and away from the jumper. To enter back door, the jumper waits until the rope reaches its peak and moves in as the rope moves downward.

The following are jumps that you can have children perform. In order, they progress from the less difficult jumps to the more challenging tasks.

▷ Jump the Stick

The turners hold the rope completely motionless, with the middle about 6 inches off the floor. The jumper stands in the middle facing one of the turners. The jumper begins by jumping sideways back and forth over the rope, completely clearing it each time. After 10 consecutive jumps, the players rotate with a turner becoming the next jumper. After the initial turn, jumpers should try jumping forward and backward 10 times (not sideways).

▷ High Water

This jump adds a little challenge to Jump the Stick. One rope turner holds the motionless rope waist level high, and the other turner holds his end to the floor. Starting at the low end, the jumper progresses up the rope, jumping higher and higher as he approaches the high end of the rope. Players rotate positions after each turn.

▷ Pendulum Jump

This jump is named after the style of rope swing that resembles the pendulum on a grandfather's clock. The turners swing the rope back and forth (half turns). Jumpers can either start in the middle or they can enter a moving rope. Players rotate positions after each turn.

▷ Run Through

The turners execute the regular full turn swing. Players take turns running through the turning rope without getting touched. Both the *Front Door* and *Back Door* entries can be introduced and performed with this activity.

▷ Regular Jumping

Jumpers attempt to jump a turning rope a predetermined number of times. Begin with the jumper in the middle, and progress to having the jumpers enter a turning rope.

▷ Jump Stunts

After the players have mastered regular jumping, consider adding some challenges such as performing quarter and half turns, touching the ground after each jump, straddle jumping, using a rocker step, etc. Also consider using challenges with equipment, such as bouncing a ball while jumping, jumping a hula hoop (like a short rope) while jumping the long rope, juggling while jumping, etc.

▷ Hot Pepper

With a jumper in the middle, the turners begin by turning the rope slowly. They progressively turn it faster and faster. The objective for the jumper is last as long as possible.

▷ The Rising Bridge

With a jumper in the middle, the turners begin by turning the rope slowly. After several turns of the rope, one of the turners (not both) gradually walks backward causing the middle of the rope to rise higher. The jumper must jump progressively higher and higher to avoid stopping the rope.

▷ Egg Beater

This challenging jump requires five players (four turners and one jumper), and two ropes. The ropes are crossed in a "+" pattern, with each end held by a turner. In unison, both ropes are turned either front door or back door. The jumper attempts to enter the turning ropes, jump a predetermined number of times, and exit without stopping the ropes.

▷ Double Dutch

This type of jumping requires two rope turners turning the ropes in opposite directions. Turners rotate the hands inward toward middle of the body with the right forearm moving counterclockwise and the left forearm clockwise. Jumpers enter by standing beside a turner and running into the ropes when the back rope (farther from the jumper) touches the floor.

▷ Jumping Rhymes

Jump rope rhymes are very popular and can help children keep rhythm, keep jump counts, and describe stunts to be performed. The following are a few that elementary-age children will enjoy at recess:

1. (Jump Counting)

    Candy, candy in the dish:
    How many pieces do you wish?
    One, Two, Three (and so on).

2. (Jump Counting)

    Tick, Tock, Tick, Tock,
    Give the time by the clock.
    It's one, two, (up to midnight).

3. (Jump Counting)

    James, James (student's name) at the gate,
    Eating cherries from a plate
    How many cherries did he eat?
    One, two, three (and so on).

4. (Jump Counting)

    Alphabet, alphabet,
    I know my A,B,C's,
    Alphabet, alphabet
    Listen to me …A, B, C, (all the way to Z).

5. (Stunt Performing)

    Teddy Bear, Teddy Bear, turn around,
    Teddy Bear, Teddy Bear, touch the ground,
    Teddy Bear, Teddy Bear, touch your shoe,
    Teddy Bear, Teddy Bear, jump turn, too
    Teddy Bear, Teddy Bear, go upstairs (lift knees high)
    Teddy Bear, Teddy Bear, say your prayers,
    Teddy Bear, Teddy Bear, turn out the lights,
    Teddy Bear, Teddy Bear, say good night (jumper exits)

6. (Stunt Performing)

    At the beach, at the sea,
    The waves come almost to the knee.
    Higher, higher (and so forth).

7. (Hot Pepper)

    James, James (student's name), set the table,
    Bring the plates if you are able,
    Don't forget the salt and
    The red hot pepper (turners turn the rope faster and
    faster).

8. (Hot Pepper)

    I like milk, I like tea,
    How many girls (or boys) are wild about me?
    One, two (and so on as the rope turns faster and faster).

Short Rope Jumping

INTRODUCTION

After children understand the rhythmical jumping required with a long rope, they usually progress rather easily to an individual rope. As with the long rope, jumping with an individual rope is packed with fitness and skill benefits. It's particularly valuable as part of the conditioning component of a physical education lesson.

NUMBER OF PLAYERS

One jump rope for each jumper; an unlimited number of jumpers can participate if space permits.

EQUIPMENT

One rope for each player (rope lengths can vary from five feet for the youngest children to nine feet for the older children).

HOW TO PLAY

Each child needs one rope with the length of the rope dependent on the height of the jumper. It should be long enough so that the ends reach the armpits or slightly higher when the child stands on its center. When children experience difficulty in jumping, it is usually a problem in the coordination of hand and foot movements. Remember that rope jumping involves two separate skills: jumping a rope and turning a rope.

Without a rope, let them practice a "pretend" jump. That is, they move the hands and practice jumping with correct rhythm and footwork. The next progression would be to hold the rope to one side with both hands, swing the rope forward and jump each time the rope hits the floor. Finally, have them progress to jumping forward and backward over a stationary rope that they hold in front of them. Gradually increase the swing until a full turn of the rope is made.

Some instructional procedures to use for improving jumping technique are as follows:

1) The body should be in good alignment, with the head up and the eyes looking straight ahead. The jump is made with the body in an erect position.

2) The rope should be held by the index finger and thumb on each side, with the elbows held near the sides of the body.

3) While turning, keep the arms at the side of the body. Many children mistakenly lift the arms trying to move the rope overhead. This makes it impossible to jump over the elevated rope.

4) Turn the rope by making small circles with the wrists.

5) The landing should be made on the balls of the feet, with the knees bent slightly to cushion the force of the jump.

6) Introduce the terms *Slow Time* and *Fast Time* when the children are ready to jump with a turn of the rope. In slow time rhythm, the player jumps over the rope, rebounds, and then executes the second jump. The rebound is simply a hop in place as the rope passes over the head. The result is two jumps for each turn. In fast time rhythm, the player jumps one time for each turn of the rope.

The following are basic jump steps. In order, they are listed from the least difficult to the more challenging.

▷ Two Foot Jump

This is often the first step children learn when introduced to the individual rope. Using either fast or slow time rhythm (see above), the player jumps over the rope with both feet together.

▷ Alternate Foot Step

In the Alternate Foot Step, the jumper alternately shifts his feet as the rope passes under the feet, resembling a running-in-place pattern.

▷ Double Side Swing Jump

Swing the rope once on each side of the body. Follow the second swing with a jump over the rope. Repeat the swing, swing, jump pattern.

▷ Bird Jumps

Similar to the Two-Foot Jump, except the player alternately jumps with the toes pointed in (as in a pigeon walk) and with the toes pointed out (as in a duck walk). Repeat the toes in, toes out pattern.

▷ Rocker Step

In performing this step, one leg is always forward in a walking-stride position. As the rope passes under the front foot, the weight is shifted from the back foot to the forward foot. Shift the weight from the front foot to the back foot after the rope passes underneath. The motion resembles that of a rocking chair going back and forth.

▷ Straddle Jump

The jumper alternates a regular jump with a straddle jump. The straddle jump is performed with the feet spread to shoulder width. After the straddle jump, the performer moves his feet back together. The motion resembles a jumping jack exercise.

▷ Mountain Climber

Start in a stride position (as in the Rocker) with one leg in front of the other. The weight should be equally distributed on both feet. As the rope passes under the feet, jump into the air and reverse the position of the feet.

▷ Mountain Skier

The performer jumps sideways, off both feet, over a line on the floor. The sideways motion resembles that of a skier moving down a mountain slope. Children should try it in a forward and backward direction also.

▷ Cross Legs Jump

The performer begins by jumping off both feet and taking the rebound in a straddle position. As the rope passes under the feet on the next turn, jump into the air and cross the feet with the right foot forward. Then repeat with the left foot forward and continue this alternation.

▷ Shuffle Step

This resembles a dance step as it involves pushing off with the right foot and sidestepping to the left as the rope passes under the feet. Land with the weight on the left foot and touch the right toes beside the left heel. Repeat the step in the opposite direction.

▷ Skipping Step

The jumper performs a step-hop (or a skip) as the rope passes under the feet.

▷ Heel-Toe Step

As the rope passes under the feet, jump with the weight landing on the left foot while touching the right heel forward. On the next turn of the rope, jump, land on the same foot, and touch the right toes beside the left heel. Repeat the pattern with the opposite foot bearing the weight.

▷ Bleking Step

The step begins with a hop on the left foot with the right heel forward, followed by a hop on the right with the left heel forward. This action is repeated with a slow-slow, fast-fast-fast pattern.

▷ Criss-Cross Jump

Start with the feet together. As the rope is turning overhead, cross the arms in front of the body to create a loop with the rope. The arms stay crossed as the player jumps through the loop. As the rope passes under the feet, the player uncrosses the arms and performs a regular two-foot jump. Repeat the alternating pattern.

▷ Double Unders

The jumper starts with a few basic two-foot jumps in preparation for the double turn. As the rope approaches the feet, the player turns the rope with a fast whip from the wrists, jumps from 4-8 inches in height, and allows the rope to pass under the feet twice before landing. The jumper should bend forward at the waist to help increase the speed of the rope. Advanced rope jumpers can be challenged to see how many consecutive double unders they can perform without stopping the rope.

Rainy Day Games

At times, the need arises to conduct recess in the classroom because of inclement weather. This section contains a variety of games and activities that can enhance fitness, movement, and academic skills in the regular classroom setting. They require very little equipment, are easy to teach, and offer a fun alternative to regular outdoor play.

Classroom Games

INTRODUCTION

The use of indoor recess games can provide an important interdisciplinary learning tool and boost to both academic and movement learning. Many of the skills which students learn during recess activities directly correlate with skills they need for success in the classroom or gymnasium. Further, these activities can help students strengthen communication skills (that is, they can learn how to lead, to take directions, to listen, and to encourage one another). These are skills that transfer directly into the regular classroom experience.

The following suggestions will help ensure that everyone enjoys a fun, well-ordered indoor recess experience when using classroom games.

- When planning your recess game activities, consider the safety precautions that must be taken to prevent injuries and accidents. In the classroom, furniture may have to be rearranged to provide sufficient space. When using balls, avoid types that might injure students or cause damage to the windows, lights, etc. Foam or lightweight cushioned balls provide a much safer alternative.

- It is important to implement an indoor quiet signal. Using a clapping pattern or a hand signal, such as a "V" or victory salute, are often effective. Before play, it should be communicated to the students the necessity of keeping their exuberance and noise under control so that their activity does not interfere with other classes.

- Try to actively involve the entire class during play. Students should spend little—if any—time sitting and waiting for opportunities to participate. Besides providing a more enjoyable experience for each student, keeping everyone as involved as possible will help reduce behavioral problems.

NUMBER OF PLAYERS
The entire classroom

EQUIPMENT
Most of the following games require very little, if any, equipment. However, see the specific game descriptions for more information.

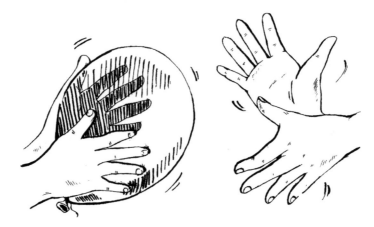

Alphabetical Numbers

The objective of this academic game is to be the first to identify which letter of the alphabet corresponds to a number that has been called out. Choose one student to be the caller. He or she begins the game by calling out any number between *1* and *26*. The other students try to be the first to find the corresponding letter of the alphabet (*1* = A, *2* = B, *7* = G, and so on). The first player with the correct answer wins a point. The game is played for a predetermined time period with the player with the most points winning. An alternative method of scoring would be to have the first player with the correct answer becoming the next caller.

VARIATION: Numbers By Letters is played with a reverse format. The caller calls out a letter, and the corresponding number must be found (A = 1, Z = 26, etc.).

Answer Scramble

This fun activity is appropriate for all grade levels and is a combination of creative movement, group cooperation, and problem solving. Divide the class into groups of 5-7 players and assign each group to a specific space within the room. The game leader begins by calling out a number or letter that each group must assemble themselves in (using all the players). The game leader can also pose questions such as "What is the first letter in our school name?" or "5 + 5 = what?" The first group to most accurately form the correct number or letter is awarded one point.

Alphabetical Words

Alphabetical Words allows children to review letters of the alphabet and become familiar with new words. Have the students form circles of 5-6 students, and distribute one ball to each circle. The activity begins with the student holding the ball calling out a word that starts with the letter A, and then he/she rolls it to another player within the circle. The next player gives a word that starts with the letter B. Play continues in this fashion until the letter Z is reached. This can be a noncompetitive game or, with older students, score can be kept and the student who is stumped the fewest times wins the game. For competitive play, a three to five second time limit should be used to call out a word.

Back to Back

This partner game is appropriate for all grade levels and does not require any equipment. With the exception of one player (the "It"), have the students stand back-to-back with a partner. The "It" starts out by calling out a command with two body parts (for example, "toe-to-toe" or "elbow-to-elbow") and then says "switch!" The players are to quickly find a new partner and touch the body parts as commanded. At the same time, the "It" finds a partner. This results in another player not having a partner (who now becomes the new "It"). Play continues with the new "It" making the next set of commands and saying "switch." Players cannot have the same partner twice during the game. The objective is to last the game without becoming an "It."

Balloon Volleyball

Students can safely play volleyball in the classroom by modifying the rules and using balloons and string in place of the regular equipment. Divide the class into two equal teams with each player seated on the floor. A string or rope is placed on the floor (or 2-3 feet off the floor) to separate the two teams. Balloon Volleyball is best played informally without most of the rules and violations of regular volleyball. The players start by hitting a balloon back and forth over the line. A point is scored if the balloon touches the floor on the opponent's side, or if the balloon fails to travel over the string. Allow the balloon to be batted an unlimited number of times by a player or team. Players are to remain seated and cannot stand up at any time during the game. After awhile, consider adding an additional balloon(s).

Basketball Scramble

This game uses basketball terminology, but does not require any equipment. Designate one student to start as the "caller." Have the rest of the students sit on the top of their desks, and give each student one of three basketball positions: guard, forward, or center (the positions should be distributed evenly). The caller starts the game by calling out one of the basketball positions. All of the players with that position must quickly change seats with one another—however, the caller must also try to find an empty seat at this same time. The one player left without a seat becomes the new caller. The game begins again with the new caller calling out a position. Make sure the positions are called out evenly and randomly.

VARIATION: Soccer Scramble and **Football Scramble** are played exactly as described above but with positions specific to these two sports. For example, in Football Scramble you would play with the positions of wide receiver, lineman, running back, quarterback, and so forth. In Soccer Scramble, you would use the positions of forward, goalie, halfback, and fullback.

Beanbag Relay

This simple relay requires only a minimal amount of classroom space and can be can with all grades. Divide the class into teams of equal numbers (5-6 players is ideal). Have the teams stand in single-file lines. The first player in each line starts with five beanbags. On a starting signal, the first player passes the beanbags one at a time over his or her shoulder to the second player in line. The second player must have all five beanbags before passing them to the third player, and so on. When the last player has received all five beanbags, all of the players immediately turn (facing the opposite direction), and the relay continues in the same manner but in reverse. The first team to successfully pass all five beanbags back to the first player wins the relay.

Buzz

Buzz is a fun mathematical game that is appropriate for 3rd through 6th graders. Divide the class into several groups. The objective for each group is to collectively count to 100 as quickly as possible while substituting the word "buzz" for the number seven, a number with seven in it (for example, "17"), or any multiple of seven (for example, "14" or "21"). The first player in each group begins by saying "One." The next player calls out "Two," and the counting continues in turn. When a player mistakenly says a number instead of "buzz," the group must starting counting at one begin.

Charades

The object of Charades is to guess, as quickly as possible, the famous phrase or sentence being acted out by teammates. Two teams are formed; one starts as the actors and the other as the audience. Each student in the audience writes down a famous saying on a slip of paper and deposits it into a bowl. An actor draws one paper at a time from the bowl and tries to convey the meaning of the phrase through gestures to his or her teammates. As the actor pantomimes, his or her teammates call out their guesses as quickly as possible. The game leader keeps track of how long it takes the team to guess the right answer each time. To ensure everyone has a chance to pantomime, set a time limit of one minute. After all the actors have had a chance to pantomime their message, they exchange roles with the audience. At the conclusion of play, the team with the least amount of guessing time wins the game.

Camel

Camel is best played in small groups (4-6 students in each group is ideal). Select one player from each group to begin as the "Guesser." The Guesser must leave the group while the other players select a secret word that the Guesser must discover. In turn, the players must make up a sentence using that word—however, each player must substitute the word "camel" for the secret word. For example, if the secret word is "sun," the players could say "When the camel comes out, the temperature rises," or "The clouds are blocking the camel." When the Guesser correctly identifies the secret word, he or she changes places with the last player to make a sentence.

Classroom Billiards

This fun game requires some string, one unsharpened pencil, and 10 golf balls for each pair of students. To begin, assign two players to a game. With string, the players make a circle on the floor that is about 3 feet in diameter. Nine golf balls are then set inside the circle; and, one golf ball (colored or marked) is designated the "cue" ball and is placed along the edge of the string. The player selected to "shoot" first takes the unsharpened pencil and uses it like a real pool cue, sliding it along the hand to push the cue ball into a golf ball. The goal is to knock as many golf balls out of the circle as possible. If a player knocks a ball out, he/she gets another turn, unless the cue ball is knocked out as well. A player can shoot until failing to knock a ball out of the circle. When this happens, the next player shoots from wherever the cue ball rolled and stopped. If the cue ball goes out of the circle, the next player can place it anywhere inside the circle. The first player to knock 5 balls out of the circle wins the game.

Classroom Bocce

Classroom Bocce is a variation of the regular game of "Marbles." However, this game is played with the strategy and rules of Bocce, a traditional Italian lawn-bowling sport. The required equipment are: 6 same-color marbles for each player; one large "target" marble for each game; and string to mark a playing area. Divide the class into groups of 2 or 3 players for each game. For multiple games, clear out as much space as possible around the classroom. Have the players design their play area by placing string on the floor to act as the shooting line. Each player is given 6 marbles of one color. One large marble is needed in each game to serve as the "target." Standing behind the shooting line, the first player flicks the large target marble into the play area. Next, the same player shoots one of his/her six marbles, aiming to land it as close as possible to the target. In turn, the other players take a shot, and play goes on until all the players have pitched their six marbles. There are no penalties for hitting other marbles or the target. (In fact, it's a good strategy to sometimes knock other players' marbles further from the target.) After all the marbles are shot, the player whose marble is closest to the target scores one point. Succeeding rounds are played the same way.

Colder & Warmer

This game can be played with all grade levels and requires only one beanbag. To begin, choose one player to be the "searcher," and have this player leave the room while the remaining players hide the beanbag. After the searcher is brought back into the room, he or she is directed to the beanbag through hints given by the other players. If the searcher is far away from the beanbag, the others say "cold." If the searcher is near the beanbag, they say "warm," then "hot," as he or she draws closer and closer. "Freezing" and "burning" are other temperature variations that can be used. Have the players take turns as the searcher.

Farm Animals

This fun game is appropriate with all grade levels and can be played with or without blindfolds. If played without blindfolds, the players should close their eyes. Before starting play, the game leader walks among the players and whispers the name of a farm animal to each one such as horse, cow, chicken, and pig. On a starting signal, the players begin moving around (with their eyes closed or blindfolded) searching for players who have the same animal name by making the sound of their specific animal ("oink," "moo," "cluck," etc.). As the players find members of their group, they join hands and move together looking for other members. The game ends when each group collects all its members together.

Geography

This challenging social studies game is best played with upper elementary-age students. Divide the class into small groups of 5-6 students and have each group play their own game. One player in each group is chosen to go first. This student begins by calling out the name of a city, state, or country. The next player in line must call the name of a city, state, or country that begins with the last letter in the name just called. For example, "New York" can be followed with "Kansas City," followed by "Yucatan," and "New Hampshire," and so forth. Any player who fails to name a city, state, or country with the appropriate letter is out. The last player left is the winner.

Gossip Relay

The object of this game is to pass a message around the group as quickly as possible and see how well the original phrase was transmitted. Divide the class into two teams. Each team forms a circle with one player in each group designated to start a "rumor." The first player quickly whispers a statement into the ear of the next player. The phrase is rapidly passed around the circle from ear to ear. The player in each team to receive the message must recite exactly what he or she heard (not an easy task!). The first team to finish and repeat the phrase correctly wins.

Ha, Ha, Ha

Ha, Ha, Ha can be played with all grade levels, and it does not require any equipment. Form groups of 5-10 students. Have each group form a circle with all the players seated. The object of the game is to avoid laughing. One player in each circle starts the game by saying "Ha"; the next player says "Ha, Ha"; the next continues with "Ha, Ha, Ha"; and so on around the circle with each player adding a "Ha." Any player who starts laughing must drop out of the circle. However, he or she can continue to make the remaining players laugh in any way except for touching. The most serious player (by keeping a straight face and not laughing) wins the game.

Hole in One

Here is a simple classroom game that approximates the hole-in-one play in golf. In Hole-in-One, players compete to "sink their shots" by rolling a marble into a cup. To start, give each player a marble and plastic cup. The cup is laid on its side (this is the "hole"), about 4-6 feet from the "tee-off" line. Players sit or crouch on the ground on the tee-off line, and each takes a turn trying to roll his/her marble into the cup. Each "hole-in-one" counts for a point. The game goes until one player reaches a predetermined score and wins the game.

Hoop Pass

Form evenly numbered groups of 6-10 students. Each group starts in a circular formation with the players holding hands. A hula hoop is given to each group and is to rest on the joined hands of two players. On a starting signal, the players attempt to pass the hoop around the circle as quickly as possible without breaking their hands apart. The hoop will be passed along by squatting and stepping through. The relay ends when the hoop has arrived back to its starting position.

I Saw

This is a fun variation of charades that children in the primary grades will enjoy. One child is selected to be the first actor. The actor starts by reciting, "This morning, on my way to school, I saw…," and then proceeds to pantomime the object or person. The other children try to guess what the actor is imitating. The child who guesses correctly becomes the leader, and the game starts again. If no one guesses correctly, the actor tells what he saw, and another actor is selected.

I Spy

This classic guessing game has been played by children for generations. Because it has few rules, it can be enjoyed by a wide range of ages. It's also very educational for younger children who are learning to identify objects, colors, and letters. To begin, choose one player to start as the "Spy." The Spy looks around chooses an object, but doesn't tell anyone. The Spy then says, "I spy something _____." The blank is filled in with the color of the chosen object. The other players now take turns guessing the object. Each takes a turn naming something with the selected color until the mystery is solved. The player who guesses correctly is the winner and gets to choose the next object.

Knots

This is a fun challenge that's appropriate for all grade levels. Form groups of 5-10 students, with the children standing close together in a circle with the arms extended. When ready, each player grasps hands with two different people on the opposite side of the circle. The grips must not be released. Once everyone's hands are linked and the group is in a "knot," the players can begin "unknotting" themselves. To accomplish this without letting go of the hands, players can crawl, step around, and step over others.

Mathematical Baseball

Create a small playing field by placing four bases about 6 to 8 feet apart in the shape of a baseball diamond. Divide the players into two equal teams. One team takes fielding positions (pitcher, catcher, first baseman, etc.), while the other team lines up in a batting order. The first batter steps up to home base and the pitcher immediately calls out a math problem. For example, "5 plus 5 equals what?" or "5 times 5 equals what?" If the batter answers correctly first, he or she advances to first base. If, however, the catcher has the correct answer first, the batter is out. The next player who comes to bat is given a problem and either advances or is called out in the same manner. Any other players on base are also advanced if the batter answers correctly. At any time, the pitcher may try to put runners out by calling out a math problem their way. If the baseman answers correctly, the runner is called out. If the base runner answers correctly, then he or she is allowed to safely "steal" a base. As in regular baseball, the teams switch roles after three outs. The team with the highest number of runs after a predetermined number of innings wins the game.

Limbo

This object of this popular activity is to walk underneath a limbo stick without touching it and, at the same time, without having the hands touch the floor. Arrange the room so that there is a large open area. Although optional, Limbo is more fun when upbeat music is played, such as Chubby Checker's hit tune from the 1960's called "Limbo Rock." Choose two students to hold the limbo stick about shoulder height. The other students form a line and, in turn, try to walk (facing upward) underneath the stick without touching it, and without falling backward causing the hands to touch the floor. A player is called out after a touch. Have the players who are called out begin a new game in another area of the classroom. After each round, select new limbo stick holders and adjust the limbo stick lower and lower. Repeat this process until only one player is left.

O'Grady Says

O'Grady Says, a variation of Simon Says (see page 180), is a fun game that can be played with all grade levels. To begin, the game leader stands in front of the class and calls out various military commands, such as "Attention," "Left face," "Right face," "About face," and "At ease." However, the players follow the commands only when first preceded by the words "O'Grady Says." Any player that moves at the wrong time is eliminated and must sit down. Nonmilitary commands involving other types of movement can also be used. For added challenge, have the game leader call out the commands as rapidly as possible.

Musical Chairs

Before starting play, make sure there is one less chair than there are students playing the game. Arrange the chairs back-to-back in two rows or in a straight line with every other chair facing in the opposite direction. Start the music and have the players march around the chairs in the same direction. When the game leader stops the music, the players are to quickly find a chair and sit down. The player left without a chair is eliminated from the game. A chair is then removed in order to keep the number of chairs one less than that of players. Continue the game, removing one chair after each round, until there are two players and one chair left. The player who gets the last chair wins.

VARIATION: Non-Elimination Musical Chairs provides an alternative to the elimination of players that is a part of regular Musical Chairs. This game is played much as described above. However, instead of eliminating the players who do not find a chair, have them sit on the knees of players who are already seated. Remove a chair or two after each stoppage of music. Continue playing until the entire class is sitting on chairs, or until there is absolutely no room left on the chairs.

Twenty Questions

The object of this game is to guess the identity of a famous person by asking for clues gained from no more than 20 questions. One player is selected to think of a well-known person. The figure can be someone from the past (for example, George Washington) or in the present (the school principal), as long as he or she is famous enough to be known by all those playing the game. One by one, the other players ask questions requiring yes or no answers that will help them discover the identity of the object. They are only allowed to ask a total of twenty questions. If a player guesses incorrectly before the twenty questions, he or she is eliminated from the game. After the players have asked a total of twenty questions and they still don't have an answer, each player is then allowed one guess. Anyone who guesses correctly becomes the starter for the next game.

Silent Speedball

This simple ball-passing game is played with the students sitting on the tops of their desks. Select two players to each start with a small foam ball. On a starting signal, the players begin tossing the balls to other players at random. Each player has three seconds in which to toss the ball to another player, and a toss to a receiver must be accurate. A toss that can not be easily caught results in the thrower being eliminated and he or she must sit down. If the receiver drops the ball, he or she must sit down. A player is also eliminated for holding on to a ball for more than three seconds. The game ends when there are only two players left.

Stairway

The game leader divides the class into four equal teams, and designates one player from each team to select a letter from which his or her team is to form a "stairway" of words. If the letter is A, a team's stairway might look like the example below. On a starting signal, the first player from each team runs to the chalk-board and writes a letter. The players, in turn, form words by adding one letter at a time to the original letter. After a given time period (five to ten minutes is ideal), the team that has built the longest stairway wins the game.

Simon Says

One player is selected to be Simon and stands in front of the class. Simon gives a variety of commands while, at the same time, demonstrating the movements. Examples include; "Clap your hands," "Touch your knees," "Turn around," "Pat your head," and so forth. However, the other players perform the movement only when the commands are preceded with the words "Simon Says." Those who move at the wrong time are eliminated and must sit out the rest of the game. The last player remaining becomes the next Simon.

Who Has the Treasure?

The object of the game is for the "hunter" to discover who has the coin and for the other players to hide the location of the coin from the "hunter." Form groups of 8-10 players. Each group is to have its players sit closely together in a circle. One player is chosen to be the "hunter" and must sit in the center of the circle. While the hunter's eyes are closed, the game leader hands one of the players in the circle a coin. The circle players begin passing (or pretending to pass) the coin around the circle without actually showing it to the hunter as he or she watches. When the hunter suspects someone of having the coin, he or she calls out the name of that player. The called player must reveal whether he or she has the coin. If this player has the coin, he or she becomes the hunter. If the hunter guesses incorrectly, the game continues.

Sports Draw

This unique game allows children to practice their artistic abilities. Divide the class into two equal teams. Designate one player from each team to stand by the chalkboard (with chalk in hand) and begin as an artist. The game leader begins by whispering a sport related object to the two artists. The artists proceed to draw the object on the chalkboard. When finished, they call upon teammates to guess what the object is. The artist may not talk or give hints. The first team to recognize and call out the name of the sport object wins the round. After each round, the game leader selects a new artist for each team. The game continues until every student has had a chance to draw.

Word Lightning

The object of this game is to think of as many words as possible beginning with a given letter in one minute. Each student pairs up with a partner. One player starts by assigning his or her partner with a letter. The partner has one minute to call out as many words as possible that begin with that letter, while the first player keeps count and watches the clock. Play continues until each player has had a turn calling out a list of words. The player with the most words wins.

Appendix

Suggested Resources

___

BOOKS

Bailey, G. *The Physical Educator's Big Book of Sport Lead-Up Games*. Camas, WA: Educators Press, 2004

Bailey, G. *The Ultimate Homeschool Physical Education Game Book*. Camas, WA: Educators Press, 2003

Bailey, G. *The Ultimate Playground & Recess Game Book*. Camas, WA: Educators Press, 2001

Barrett, B. *Games For The Whole Child*. Champaign, IL: Human Kinetics, 2005

Brooking-Payne, K. *Games Children Play*. Gloucestershire, England: Hawthorne Press, 1996

Byl, J. *Co-Ed Recreational Games*. Champaign, IL: Human Kinetics, 2002

Carr, T. *Games From Long Ago & Far Away*. West Nyack, NY: Parker Publishing Co., 2001

Dieden, B. *Games To Keep Kids Moving!* West Nyack, NY: Parker Publishing Co., 1995

Dowson, A. & Morris, K. *Fun and Games*. Champaign, IL: Human Kinetics, 2005

Drake, J. & Love, A. *The Kids Summer Games Book*. Tonawanda, NY: Kids Can Press Ltd., 1998

Hinson, C. *Fitness for Children*. Champaign, IL: Human Kinetics, 1995

Hinson, C. *Games Kids Should Play at Recess*. Wilmington, DE: The Physical Education Resources Co., 1997

Launder, A. *Play Practice*. Champaign, IL: Human Kinetics, 2001

MacGregor, C. *Everybody Wins!*. Avon, MA: Adams Media Corp., 1998

Maguire, J. *Hopscotch, Hangman, Hot Potato, & Ha Ha Ha*. New York, NY: Simon & Schuster, 1990

Orlick, T. *The Second Cooperative Sports and Games Book*. New York, NY: Pantheon Books, 1982

Pangrazi, R. *Dynamic Physical Education for Elementary School Children*. 13d ed. Boston, MA: Allyn & Bacon, 2001

Pellegrini, A.D. *Recess*. Mahwah, NJ: Lawrence Erlbaum Publishers, 2005

Steffins, C. & Gorin, S. *Learning to Play, Playing to Learn*. Los Angeles, CA: Lowell House, 1997

Sweet, J. *365 Activities for Fitness, Food, and Fun for the Whole Family*. New York, NY McGraw-Hill, 2001

West, B. *Celebration Games*. Champaign, IL: Human Kinetics, 2006

ORGANIZATIONS

American Alliance for Health, Physical Education, Recreation and Dance (AAHPERD)
1900 Association Drive
Reston, VA 22091-1599
(800) 213-7193
www.aahperd.org

American Council On Exercise
5820 Oberlin Drive, #102
San Diego, CA 92121
www.acefitness.org

Australian Council for Health, Physical Education, Recreation, Inc. (ACHPER)
214 Port Road
Hindmarsh, Australia 5007
(08) 8340-3388
www.achper.org.au

Canadian Association for Health, Physical Education, Recreation and Dance (CAHPERD)
403-2197 Riverside Drive
Ottawa, Ontario K1H 7X3
(613) 523-1348
www.cahperd

National Association for Health & Fitness
65 Niagara Square, Rm. 607
Buffalo, NY 14202
(716) 583-0521
www.physicalfitness.org

National Program for Playground Safety
School for Health, Physical Education and Leisure Services
WRC 205
University of Northern Iowa
Cedar Hills, IA 50614
(319) 273-2416
www.uni.edu/playground

National Youth Sports Safety Foundation, Inc.
333 Longwood Avenue, Suite 202
Boston, MA 02115
(617) 277-1171
www.nyssf.org

President's Council on Physical Fitness and Sports
Dept. W
200 Independence Avenue SW
Room 738-H
Washington, DC 20201-0004
(202) 690-9000
www.fitness.gov

Youth Fitness Resource Center
PO Box 5076
Champaign, IL 61825-5076
www.americanfitness.net

YMCA of the USA
Association Advancement
101 North Wacker Drive
Chicago, IL 60606
(312) 977-0031
www.ymca.net

YWCA
1015 18th Street NW, Suite 1100
Washington, DC 20036
(202) 467-0801
www.ywca.org

OTHER WEBSITES OF NOTE

Family Friendly Fun and Life Resources
www.family-friendly-fun.com

PE Central
www.pecentral.com

PlayFit Education Inc.
www.playfiteducation.com

Games Kids Play
www.gameskidsplay.net

World Playground Web Directory
www.world-playground.com

Index

(alphabetical by game)

**The true object of all human life is play.
Earth is a task garden: heaven is a playground.**

-G.K. Chesterton, British author (1936)

About the Author

Guy Bailey, M.Ed., has over 24 years of experience teaching physical education at the elementary and middle school levels. During this time, he also directed the after-school sport activities at various schools and coached numerous youth sports on the side. His educational background includes having a B.S. degree (Central Washington University), and a M.Ed. degree (Portland State University) in his specialty area of physical education.

In addition to this book, Guy has authored four other popular books on physical education. *Gym Scooter Fun & Games*, released in 2007, is a one-of-a-kind resource devoted to gym scooter play in grades K-8. *The Ultimate Playground & Recess Game Book* is a special collection of over 170 playground and recess activities for K-6 grade children. *The Physical Educator's Big Book of Sport Lead-Up Games* is a comprehensive resource of games used to develop sport skills, and has been adopted by many college professors throughout the country as a required text for their courses. *The Ultimate Homeschool Physical Education Game Book* is a unique collection of partner and small group games aimed at helping home educators teach physical education skills to children in the home and backyard setting.

During his career as a physical educator, Guy's professional goal was to equip each of his students with a love of movement and the basic skills needed to participate in an active lifestyle now and later as adults. He believes that for lasting skill learning to take place, physical education needs to consist of success-oriented learning experiences that literally leave children craving for more. This book reflects Guy's philosophy of using activities—both in the gymnasium and on the playground— that are not only skill based, but fun and meaningful as well.

In addition to his teaching and writing endeavors, Guy is actively involved in promoting literacy among elementary-age children. He has spoken at school assemblies on the subject of authoring books, and has worked with various community groups on motivating children to read more often.

Guy resides in Vancouver, Washington. He has three sons, Justin, Austin, Carson, and a daughter, Heather. In his spare time, he enjoys reading, writing, jogging, weightlifting, fishing, and hiking the various trails in the beautiful Columbia River Gorge near his home. He also has a passion for college athletics and is a frequent visitor to college stadiums and gymnasiums throughout the Pacific Northwest.

Guy is an active member of the American Alliance of Health, Physical Education, Recreation and Dance.

Ordering Information

Please contact your favorite educational catalog company or local bookstore to order additional copies of *Recess Success!* Customers can also order directly from Educators Press by using the contact information listed below. The retail cost is $21.95 per book plus $5.95 shipping (add $1 shipping for each additional book ordered). Washington state residents please add $1.78 per book for sales tax.

The following books are also available from Educators Press:

▶ **The Physical Educator's Big Book of Sport Lead-Up Games**
ISBN-10: 0966972759
ISBN-13: 978-0-9669727-5-7
$29.95 Retail Price

▶ **The Ultimate Homeschool Physical Education Game Book**
ISBN-10: 0966972740
ISBN-13: 978-0-9669727-4-0
$19.95 Retail Price

▶ **Gym Scooter Fun & Games**
ISBN-13: 978-0-9669727-7-1
$15.95 Retail Price

Credit card purchases can be made through Educators Press by calling toll-free:

1-800-431-1579

All of our titles are available at special discounts for retailers, bookstores, distributors, sales promotions, and premium sale programs. For details, contact the sales manager at Educators Press by telephone at (360) 597-4355, fax (360) 326-1606, or by email at educatorspress@att.net.

EDUCATORS PRESS

15610 NE 2nd Street
Vancouver, WA 98684
(T) 360-597-4355   (F) 360-326-1606
www.educatorspress.com

The Library Store #47-0119